Cambridge National

Sport Studies

If you want to succeed at the Cambridge National in Sport Studies, there's only one thing for it — lots and lots of practice. Luckily for you, this CGP book is brimming with it!

It guides you through all the different question types in the final exam (Unit R184: Contemporary Issues in Sport), with lots of realistic practice questions to help you prepare.

We've also included fully worked answers to check how you've done and see where to improve — perfect for making sure you're ready for the exam!

Unlock your Online Edition

Just scan the QR code below or go to **cgpbooks.co.uk/extras** and enter this code!

3619 6976 8955 5257

By the way, this code only works for one person. If somebody else has used this book before you, they might have already claimed the code.

Exam Practice Workbook

Contents

Exam Skills 1

Section 1 — Short & Medium-Answer Questions

Exam Skills 2

Published by CGP

Editors: Liam Dyer, Sharon Keeley-Holden, Adam Worster

Author: Carl Attwood
Reviewer: Chris Cope

With thanks to Mary Falkner and Sheryl Gayle for the proofreading.
With thanks to Jan Greenway for the copyright research.

ISBN: 978 1 83774 059 8
Printed by Elanders Ltd, Newcastle upon Tyne.

Short & Medium-Answer Questions

You'll sit a written exam that's worth **70 marks**.
It lasts **1 hour and 15 minutes** and counts for **40%** of your total grade.

Section A contains **short and medium-answer questions**, including some **multiple-choice questions**.

Section B and **Section C** include **short and medium-answer questions**, plus an **extended-response question** (see p.37).

Short and medium-answer questions usually begin with these **command words**:

- **Which...**
- **Draw...**
- **State...**
- **Identify...**
- **Describe...**
- **Explain...**

'Which...' and 'Draw...' questions are usually multiple-choice

For '**Which**' and '**Draw**' questions, you just need to pick out the correct information.
You might have to put a **tick** next to your answer or **draw lines** to show your answers.

The question tells you **how many** answers you need to give.

Put a **tick** in the box next to your answer.

1 Which **one** of the following is a negative effect of technology in sport?

- ☐ It can make sport more accessible.
- ☐ It lowers the risk of injury to performers.
- ☑ It can increase pressure on officials.
- ☐ It can increase the safety of performers.

[1]

2 Draw lines to match the **three** sporting values to the correct definition.

Sporting value
Excellence
Inclusion
Fair play

Description
Adhering to the rules and showing respectful behaviour to opponents.
Offering equal opportunities to all user groups to participate in sport.
Striving to be the best through high-level performances.
Feeling united with the whole population in support of a country.

[3]

Draw lines to show your answers.

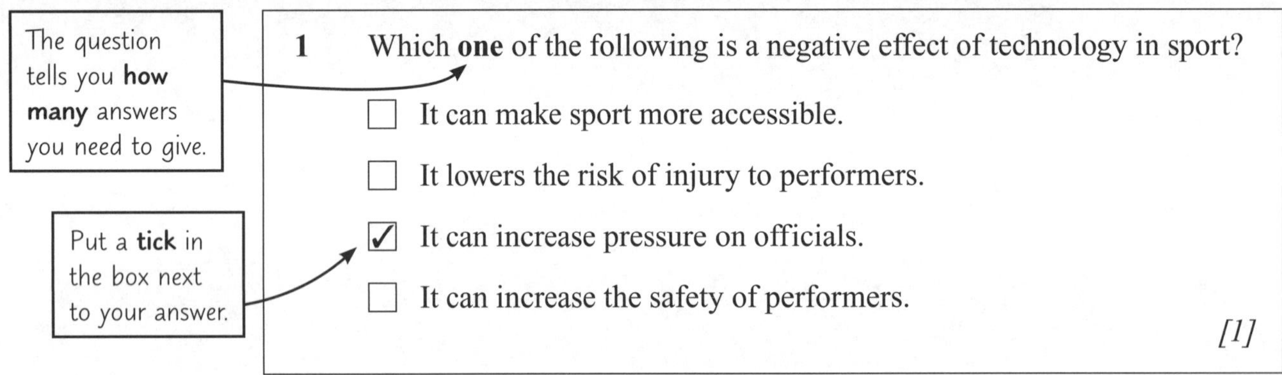

Some options might not match up — watch out for these 'distracting' answers.

Short & Medium-Answer Questions

'State...' and 'Identify...' are similar command words

For '**State**' and '**Identify**' questions, you only need to write a **few words** or a **short sentence** for each **mark** in the question. You might need to provide **examples**, **definitions** or **reasons**.

> Polly is retired and has a visual impairment.
> She has no children but often provides care for her sister's grandchildren.

Most Section B questions have a **context**.

3   Identify **three** barriers to participation in sport that Polly may face.

1. *Family commitments*
2. *Lack of positive sporting role models*
3. *Lack of appropriate activity provision*

[3]

Here, you'll get **1 mark** for each correct response you give.

'Describe...' questions need more detailed answers

The number of marks for a '**Describe**' question varies — generally, questions worth more marks will need **more detail**.

'Other than...' means you **can't** include information that is given in the question.

4   Other than lobbying other organisations for funding, describe **one** role of a National Governing Body (NGB).

There's another 'Describe' example on the next page.

An NGB will provide support and guidance to its members, such as advice on insurance.

[1]

Give reasons for 'Explain...' questions

For '**Explain**' questions, you will be expected to write about **how** or **why** something happens.

'Describe' and 'Explain' questions often ask for **practical** or **sporting examples** to show you can **apply** your knowledge.

5   Explain **two** ways in which technology benefits sports performers. For each way, give a sporting example.

Way 1: *Technology can enhance performance by making performers move more quickly.*

Sporting example: *Aerodynamic skinsuits in cycling reduce air resistance to help cyclists travel more efficiently at high speed.*

Way 2: *Assistive technology helps to make sport more accessible for people with disabilities.*

Sporting example: *Sports wheelchairs for basketball are modified wheelchairs that are more stable and can make sharper turns.*

This question is 4 marks — that's 1 mark for each **way** and 1 mark for each **linked example** you give.

[4]

Answering Short & Medium-Answer Questions

Here are two different answers to a 4-mark question

Read through the question and the sample answers below.
Then look at the explanations of **how many marks** they would get and **why**.

---

1   Describe **two** negative aspects of hosting a major sporting event.
For each aspect, give a sporting example.

Aspect 1: _The host country gets negative media coverage if the event is poorly organised._

Example: _Some countries that hosted the Olympic Games have experienced this._

Aspect 2: _People that live in the host city will benefit from the improved infrastructure._

Example: _The Copper Box Arena, built for London 2012, offers exercise classes for local people._

[4]

This answer gets **1** mark(s) out of 4, because _one suitable negative aspect of hosting a sporting event has been identified (negative media coverage), but the sporting example is not specific enough. The second aspect and example gets no marks because it is a positive aspect of hosting, not a negative aspect, so it isn't relevant to this question._

---

1   Describe **two** negative aspects of hosting a major sporting event.
For each aspect, give a sporting example.

Aspect 1: _The host country gets negative media coverage if the event is poorly organised._

Example: _Rio was criticised for failing to clean up its coastal area as part of its Olympic bid._

Aspect 2: _There is an increased risk of terrorism and crime in the host city._

Example: _England and Italy fans violently clashed at Wembley before the EURO 2020 final._

[4]

This answer gets **4** mark(s) out of 4, because _the answer gives two different negative aspects of hosting a sporting event (negative media coverage, potential for terrorism and crime), with two specific sporting examples. Each example is clearly linked to the negative aspect._

Answering Short & Medium-Answer Questions

Now it's your turn to be the examiner. Read this exam question and the sample answer.

> **2** Other than excellence and inclusion, explain **two** sporting values.
> Give an example of each value, using a named sport.
>
> Value 1: *Courage is showing what can be achieved when you push your body to its limit.*
>
> Sporting example: *Competing in the 100m sprint final at the Olympic Games.*
>
> Value 2: *Citizenship is about creating links in the local community.*
>
> Sporting example: *Volunteering at a sports club.*
>
> *[4]*

How many marks would **you** give this answer?
Explain **why** you've decided on this mark in the box below.

> I would give this answer ...... mark(s) out of 4, because ....
>
> ....
>
> ....
>
> ....

Compare what you've written to the explanation on p.68.

Now have a go at improving the answer above so that it would get **4 marks**.
Write your answer in the box below.

> **2** Other than excellence and inclusion, explain **two** sporting values.
> Give an example of each value, using a named sport.
>
> Value 1: ....
>
> Sporting example: ....
>
> ....
>
> Value 2: ....
>
> Sporting example: ....
>
> ....
>
> *[4]*

Have a look at our sample answer on p.68. **Don't worry** if your answer wouldn't have
got 4 marks — the next section gives you **a lot more practice** at these sorts of question.

User Groups

1 Draw lines to match the **four** user groups to the correct description.

User group		Description
Retired people		Adults or children who care for family members.
Carers		People who do not have a job.
Economically disadvantaged people		A single person or couple raising children.
Parents		People who no longer work and may receive money from a pension.
		People who have a long-term health condition.
		People who have a lack of disposable income.

[4]

People with disabilities is an example of a user group who participate in sport.

2 Which **one** of the following statements is true?

☐ Team sports are unsuitable for people in this user group.

☐ Everyone in this user group uses a wheelchair.

☐ Some people in this user group have a disability that is not visible.

☐ People in this user group all have a physical impairment.

[1]

3 Identify **three** user groups which are based on family structures.

1. ....

2. ....

3. ....

[3]

User Groups

4   Which **one** of the following user groups could a person
who works full-time in the UK also belong to?

     ☐   Young children

     ☐   Unemployed people

     ☐   Retired people

     ☐   Parents

[1]

5   Explain why **two** named user groups may need activity provision during the daytime on weekdays.

User group 1: ....

Explanation: ....

....

User group 2: ....

Explanation: ....

....

[4]

A person's age can affect their requirements for sport.

6   (a)   Identify a user group which is made up of people within a certain age range.

....

[1]

     (b)   State **two** possible needs of this user group when participating in sport.

1. ....

....

2. ....

....

[2]

Exam Tip

There are 12 user groups you are expected to know for your Cambridge National in Sport Studies. However, the people in any one of these user groups are likely to have wildly differing circumstances and also belong to other groups.

Barriers to Participation

1 Draw lines to match the **three** barriers to participation in sport to a possible solution.

Barrier to participation
Lack of disposable income
Lack of awareness of appropriate activity provision
Lack of positive sporting role models from minority ethnic groups

Solution
Increase the diversity of coaches and sports leaders.
Provide a wide range of activities for children so they are likely to find something that is appealing.
Introduce discounts for unemployed people who may struggle to afford fees.
Advertise activities for teenagers on social media where teenagers are likely to see these adverts.

[3]

Young children may be prevented from participating in sport by a lack of money or transport.

2 Other than the lack of money or transport, explain **one** barrier
to participation that a young child may face.

....

....

....

....

[2]

Some people who work have plenty of disposable income but still struggle to participate in sport.

3 Which **one** of the following strategies is most likely to enable them to participate?

☐ Provide reduced-price equipment hire.

☐ Provide free cycle hire.

☐ Provide sessions at a range of times.

☐ Provide taster sessions for activities.

[1]

Barriers to Participation

4   Explain and give a practical example for each of the following barriers to participation in sport.

Lack of equal coverage of different genders by the media

Explanation: ....

....

Practical example: ....

....

Lack of family support

Explanation: ....

....

Practical example: ....

....

Family commitments

Explanation: ....

....

Practical example: ....

....

[6]

5   Identify **one** way that sports facilities could be made more accessible for the following people.
(a)   A wheelchair user.

....

[1]

(b)   A partially-sighted user.

....

[1]

(c)   A hearing-impaired user.

....

[1]

Short & Medium-Answer Questions — Topic Area 1

Barriers to Participation

A lack of transport may affect participation in sport.

6 (a) Other than young children, explain how **one** user group may be prevented from participating by a lack of transport.

User group: ....

Explanation: ....

....

[2]

(b) Identify **one** solution to the barrier named in part (a).

....

....

[1]

7 Describe **two** ways that media coverage of sport may present a barrier to participation for people from minority ethnic groups.

Way 1: ....

....

....

Way 2: ....

....

....

[2]

Kailash is 75 years old and retired.

8 Identify **one** barrier to participation in sport that Kailash may face and **one** possible solution to the barrier you have identified.

Barrier: ....

....

Solution: ....

....

[2]

Barriers to Participation

Promotion strategies can be used to overcome barriers to participation in sport.

9 (a) Identify **three** promotion strategies.

1. ....

2. ....

3. ....

[3]

(b) State what is meant by targeted promotion.

....

....

[1]

(c) Explain how targeted promotion could overcome
a barrier to participation for a named user group.

....

....

....

....

[2]

Unemployment can present a barrier to participation in sport.

10 (a) State **one** reason why this is.

....

....

[1]

(b) Identify **one** solution to this barrier.

....

....

[1]

Popularity of Sport

1 Which **one** of the following is likely to negatively impact the popularity of a sport in the UK?

  ☐ The number of positive role models participating in the sport increases.

  ☐ There is a large amount of media coverage of the sport.

  ☐ The national team performs well in that sport at the Olympic Games.

  ☐ There are few opportunities to watch the sport being performed.

[1]

2 Using sporting examples, explain how **four** different factors can positively impact the popularity of sport in the UK.

Factor 1: ....

Explanation: ....

....

....

Factor 2: ....

Explanation: ....

....

....

Factor 3: ....

Explanation: ....

....

....

Factor 4: ....

Explanation: ....

....

....

[8]

Popularity of Sport

The popularity of snow sports is influenced by the environment and climate.

3 Other than a snow sport, identify **one** sport and explain how
the environment or climate impacts its popularity in the UK.

Sport: ....

Explanation: ....

....

....

[2]

4 State **three** reasons why media coverage of a sport can positively impact its popularity.

1. ....

....

2. ....

....

3. ....

....

[3]

5 State **two** examples, using named sports, where a high-level
success impacted the popularity of that sport.

1. ....

....

2. ....

....

[2]

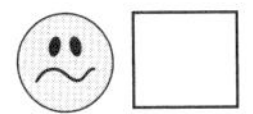  

Short & Medium-Answer Questions — Topic Area 1

Popularity of Sport

6   (a)   Explain how a named sporting role model has increased the popularity of a sport.

....

....

....

....

[2]

     (b)   Describe why it is important to have a diverse range of role models in sport.

....

....

[1]

7   State **two** reasons why a sport being added to the Olympic Games is likely
to have a positive impact on the number of participants in that sport.

Reason 1: ....

....

Reason 2: ....

....

[2]

8   State **two** reasons why a sport may not be considered socially acceptable.
For each reason, give a sporting example.

Reason 1: ....

....

Sporting example: ....

....

Reason 2: ....

....

Sporting example: ....

....

[4]

Emerging and New Sports in the UK

1 Which **one** of the following statements is true?

☐ An emerging sport is a sport which has not been around for very long.

☐ Table tennis is an example of an emerging sport in the UK.

☐ An emerging sport is a sport which is significantly gaining popularity in a country.

☐ An emerging sport never has an NGB.

[1]

2 Identify **one** example of an emerging sport in the UK and
state **two** reasons why its popularity is increasing.

Emerging sport: ....

Reason 1: ....

....

Reason 2: ....

....

[3]

3 State **three** different actions that the NGB of an emerging sport can take to develop the sport.
For each action, explain why it is likely to increase participation in the sport.

Action 1: ....

Explanation: ....

....

Action 2: ....

Explanation: ....

....

Action 3: ....

Explanation: ....

....

[6]

 ☐  ☐  ☐

Sporting Values

1   Draw lines to match the **four** sporting values to the correct description.

Sporting value		Description
Tolerance and respect		Adhering to the rules.
Citizenship		Equal opportunities for all social groups to participate in sport.
Inclusion		Striving to be the very best and working with maximum effort.
National pride		The unity of the whole population in support of the country's team or squad.
		Creating community links and spirit through involvement in local sports clubs and teams.
		Developing an understanding of other cultures.

[4]

2   Describe **two** examples which demonstrate the sporting value of inclusion.

1. ....

....

2. ....

....

[2]

3   Which **one** of the following is **not** an example of the sporting value of citizenship?

☐ Volunteering to coach a junior hockey team at the club where you play.

☐ Wearing Rainbow Laces to show support of LGBTQ+ people in sport.

☐ Joining your local badminton club.

☐ Attending a fundraising barbecue in aid of a school football team.

[1]

Sporting Values

4 State **one** practical example of how **performers** can show each of the following sporting values.

Fair play

....

....

Team spirit

....

....

Excellence

....

....

Tolerance and respect

....

....

[4]

National pride can be shown by spectators waving their country's flag or singing their national anthem at an international sporting event.

5 (a) State **one** other example of how national pride can be shown during a sporting event.

....

....

[1]

(b) State **one** example of how spectators at a sporting event can show tolerance and respect.

....

....

[1]

Exam Tip

There are seven sporting values that you need to know — make sure you can rattle them off from memory, and have lots of examples up your sleeve. Remember, tolerance AND respect are one value, so never list them separately.

Short & Medium-Answer Questions — Topic Area 2

The Olympic and Paralympic Movement

1 Which **one** of the following is the correct set of Paralympic values?

☐ Inspiration, excellence, friendship and respect.

☐ Excellence, equality, identity and fair play.

☐ Citizenship, determination, national pride and friendship.

☐ Equality, courage, inspiration and determination.

[1]

2 Explain what is meant by the Olympic creed.

....

....

....

....

[2]

The Olympic Games has a symbol to represent its identity.

3 (a) Describe the Olympic Games symbol.

....

....

[1]

(b) Explain how this symbol represents the identity of the event.

....

....

....

....

[2]

(c) Explain why friendship is an important Olympic value.

....

....

....

....

[2]

The Olympic and Paralympic Movement

> A performer at the Olympic Games can show respect to other performers
> by shaking hands with opponents at the end of a competition.

4   Identify **two** other ways a performer at the Olympic Games can show respect.
For each way, give a practical example.

Way 1: ....

....

Practical example: ....

....

Way 2: ....

....

Practical example: ....

....

[4]

5   Identify each of the Paralympic values described below.

Showing what can be achieved when you push your body to its limit.

....

*Showing mental strength, physical ability and agility to achieve things
that most people would think were impossible.*

....

*Showing that differences can be a strength, while also challenging stereotypes
and the discrimination shown towards people with disabilities.*

....

[3]

Exam Tip

There are 3 Olympic values and 4 Paralympic ones — and both sets are totally different, which seems a bit odd to me.
The official descriptions can take some getting to grips with, but you don't need to learn each definition word-for-word.

Short & Medium-Answer Questions — Topic Area 2

Sporting Initiatives

1   Which **one** of the following phrases is **not** true of a local sporting initiative?

☐ It usually operates on a small scale.

☐ It is often run by volunteers.

☐ It may be funded by a city or town council.

☐ It usually has access to large amounts of funding.

[1]

2   Identify **one** sporting initiative that promotes each of the following values.
Give **one** example of how your named initiative promotes this value.

Fair play

Sporting initiative: ....

Example: ....

....

Inclusion

Sporting initiative: ....

Example: ....

....

[4]

Sporting initiatives can be local, regional or national.

3   (a)   State the name of a regional or national sporting initiative. Give its target group.

Initiative: ....

Target group: ....

[2]

(b)   Explain whether this initiative is regional or national.

....

....

[1]

Sporting Behaviour

1   Which **one** of the following statements is true?

☐ Gamesmanship and sportsmanship mean the same thing.

☐ Showing good sportsmanship upholds the spirit of the game.

☐ Taking PEDs is an example of gamesmanship.

☐ Sportsmanship involves bending the rules to gain an advantage.

[1]

2   State why gamesmanship does not usually result in being penalised by an official.

....

....
[1]

3   Draw lines to match the **three** types of behaviour to the correct example.

Behaviour
Sportsmanship
Gamesmanship
Spectator etiquette

Example
Fans applauding skilful performances of both teams.
Wearing aerodynamic clothing for a cycling race.
A footballer time-wasting before a goal kick.
Fans cheering when a golfer misses an easy putt.
A tennis player owning up if they return a ball after a double bounce.

[3]

Exam Tip

In matching questions, there might be 'spare' definitions or examples that don't match up. Even if you think you've spotted the ones that match, it's a good idea just to check through the other options, to double check you're correct.

Short & Medium-Answer Questions — Topic Area 2

Sporting Behaviour

Many gamesmanship techniques involve breaking the flow of the game or distracting opponents.

4 State **one** example of a gamesmanship technique which involves each of these things.

Breaking the flow of the game

....

....

Distracting opponents

....

....

[2]

5 Identify **three** reasons why it is important for spectators to show good etiquette.
For each reason, give a practical example of spectator behaviour.

Reason 1: ....

....

Practical example: ....

....

Reason 2: ....

....

Practical example: ....

....

Reason 3: ....

....

Practical example: ....

....

[6]

Sporting Behaviour

Showing good sportsmanship reinforces sporting values.

6 (a) Explain what is meant by sportsmanship.

....

....

....

[2]

(b) Identify **one** example of how sportsmanship can reinforce the following sporting values.

Team spirit

....

....

Fair play

....

....

[2]

7 (a) Describe **two** sporting examples of how poor behaviour from **performers** can impact safety.

1. ....

....

2. ....

....

[2]

(b) Describe **two** sporting examples of how poor behaviour from **spectators** can impact safety.

1. ....

....

2. ....

....

[2]

> **Exam Tip**
>
> Examples, examples, examples — that's what a lot of exam questions want. Remember to name the sport you're referring to in an example when the question tells you to use 'a named sport' (unless you want to chuck marks away).

Short & Medium-Answer Questions — Topic Area 2

Performance Enhancing Drugs

1   Which **one** of the following is **not** a reason why performers
may take Performance Enhancing Drugs (PEDs)?

☐ To increase their chances of winning.

☐ They think other competitors are taking PEDs.

☐ To improve their overall health.

☐ To improve their performance.

[1]

2   State **two** negative impacts of the use of PEDs on performers and on sport.

Negative impacts on performers

1. ....

....

2. ....

....

Negative impacts on sport

1. ....

....

2. ....

....

[4]

Education strategies can help prevent the use of PEDs in sport.

3   (a)   Identify **one** education strategy which discourages the use of PEDs in sport.

....

[1]

      (b)   Explain why these education strategies often involve role models.

....

....

....

....

[2]

Performance Enhancing Drugs

WADA is an organisation involved with sport.

4 (a) State the full name of WADA.

....

[1]

(b) State **two** responsibilities of WADA.

1. ....

....

2. ....

....

[2]

5 Which **one** of the following is **not** true for WADA's Whereabouts Rule?

☐ Performers can only be tested during competitions.

☐ Performers do not know which date they will be tested.

☐ Performers must provide details about their location.

☐ Performers choose a 1-hour time slot each day to be available for testing.

[1]

6 State **two** different types of sanction for performers who have been found to have taken PEDs. For each type, give a sporting example with a named elite performer.

Sanction 1: ....

Example: ....

....

Sanction 2: ....

Example: ....

....

[4]

Exam Tip

WADA is a major player in the fight against PEDs, so make sure you know who they are and their key weapon (AKA the Whereabouts Rule). And learn the reasons why performers still take PEDs, even though they're pretty damaging.

Short & Medium-Answer Questions — Topic Area 2

Types of Sporting Event

1   Draw lines to match the **three** sporting events to the correct type.

Sporting event
Winter Paralympic Games
UEFA Champions League Final
Wimbledon

Type of sporting event
Regular event
One-off event
Regular and recurring event
Community event

[3]

2   State how the following events are scheduled:

One-off event: ....

....

Regular and recurring event: ....

....

[2]

3   Describe what is meant by a regular major sporting event, using an example.

....

....

....

....

[2]

4   State why the Olympic Games can be described as an 'international' event.

....

....

[1]

Hosting Sporting Events

1 Which **one** of the following is **not** a benefit of hosting a major sporting event?

☐ Improved national morale

☐ Increased traffic and litter

☐ Increased tourism

☐ Improved infrastructure

[1]

2 (a) State what is meant by direct tourism.

....

....
[1]

(b) Explain **one** way that direct tourism would affect the host city of a major sporting event.

....

....
[1]

Before a major sporting event, the host country will build infrastructure.

3 (a) State **three** examples of infrastructure that may be built.

1. ....

2. ....

3. ....
[3]

(b) Other than infrastructure development, identify **two** positive pre-event aspects of hosting a major sporting event.

1. ....

....

2. ....

....
[2]

> **Exam Tip**
>
> Hosting a sporting event has three stages — 'pre-event' (including bidding), 'during the event' and 'post-event'.
> You need to know the benefits and drawbacks of each stage and have plenty of real-world examples to hand too.

Short & Medium-Answer Questions — Topic Area 3

Hosting Sporting Events

4 Which **one** of the following is a possible post-event drawback of hosting a sporting event?

- [ ] Existing buildings are demolished to build new infrastructure.
- [ ] Many temporary jobs are created.
- [ ] National interest and participation in sport is increased.
- [ ] Taxes are raised if costs were more than the revenue generated.

[1]

5 Identify **three** drawbacks of bidding to host a major sporting event.

1. ....

....

2. ....

....

3. ....

....

[3]

6 Describe **one** possible positive impact and **one** possible negative impact
of increased media coverage for the host country of a sporting event.

Positive impact: ....

....

Negative impact: ....

....

[2]

7 State **two** long-term positive aspects for a host country following a successful sporting event.

1. ....

....

2. ....

....

[2]

Hosting Sporting Events

8   Draw lines to match the **three** impacts of hosting a sporting event to the correct example.

Impact of hosting a sporting event
Improved infrastructure
Increased profile of sport
Unused sporting facilities

Example
Athens 2004 Olympics: many venues used for Olympic events are now abandoned.
Sochi 2014 Olympics: Russia accused of running a doping programme.
London 2012 Olympics: upgrades and new services on the London Underground.
Tokyo 2020 Olympics: skateboarding makes its debut appearance at the Olympics.

[3]

9   Explain **one** way, using an example, that a major sporting event can impact the morale of the host nation.

....

....

....

....

[2]

10   Identify **two** reasons why residents might object to their city bidding for a major sporting event.

1. ....

....

2. ....

....

[2]

Exam Tip

Hosting the Olympics brings loads of benefits and drawbacks — it's a great example to fall back on in the exam.
Always refer to a specific event though, e.g. London 2012, Tokyo 2020 — 'the Olympics' won't cut it in your answers.

Short & Medium-Answer Questions — Topic Area 3

Hosting Sporting Events

11 State **one** positive aspect and **one** negative aspect for a host city of
receiving an increased number of visitors during a major sporting event.

Positive aspect: ....

....

Negative aspect: ....

....

[2]

Some major sporting events are hit with scandals and controversies.

12 Explain, giving an example, how a scandal can affect the host country of a major sporting event.

Explanation: ....

....

Example: ....

....

[2]

13 State **three** benefits that the host nation of a major sporting event may
experience during the event. For each benefit, give an example.

Benefit 1: ....

....

Example: ....

....

Benefit 2: ....

....

Example: ....

....

Benefit 3: ....

....

Example: ....

....

[6]

National Governing Bodies

1   Which **one** of the following describes what a National Governing Body (NGB) is?

☐ A company that controls the media rights to every sport.

☐ An international organisation that manages all major sports.

☐ A charity that works to get older people playing sport.

☐ An organisation that manages a specific sport in a country.

[1]

2   Other than by developing initiatives, identify **two** ways that a
National Governing Body can increase participation in their sport.

1. ....

....

2. ....

....

[2]

3   (a)   Identify **four** sources of funding for National Governing Bodies.

1. ....

2. ....

3. ....

4. ....

[4]

(b)   State **three** reasons why National Governing Bodies need funding.

1. ....

....

2. ....

....

3. ....

....

[3]

Exam Tip

In the exam, you might need to write about the roles of an NGB, using real-world examples. You'll be free to choose any relevant NGB — digging about on your favourite NGB's website can help you get the info you need.

 ☐    ☐    ☐

National Governing Bodies

4   Describe **three** positive impacts of a successful tournament
organised by a National Governing Body.

1. ....

....

2. ....

....

3. ....

....

[3]

One role of a National Governing Body is to enforce the rules of their sport.

5   (a)   State **two** disciplinary measures a National Governing Body may use when rules are broken.

1. ....

....

2. ....

....

[2]

(b)   Other than to increase the safety of participants, state **one** reason why the rules of a
sport may be changed. Give an example of a rule that has changed for this reason.

Reason: ....

....

Example: ....

....

[2]

6   Describe **two** reasons why it is important that a National Governing Body
develops officiating infrastructure in their sport.

1. ....

....

2. ....

....

[2]

National Governing Bodies

Clubs and individuals can access support from their National Governing Body.

7   Using examples, explain **two** types of support that a club or individual member of a National Governing Body might access.

Type of support 1: ....

....

....

Type of support 2: ....

....

....

[4]

'Survive. Revive. Thrive.' is an FA initiative to increase participation in football.

8   (a)   Identify **one** initiative from a different NGB that aims to improve participation in their sport.

....

[1]

    (b)   Describe how your chosen initiative helps to improve participation.

....

....

[1]

9   Other than safeguarding policies, state **two** ways a National Governing Body can improve the safety of participants. For each way, give a sporting example.

Way 1: ....

Example: ....

....

Way 2: ....

Example: ....

....

[4]

> **Exam Tip**
>
> A typical mistake for these NGB questions is giving an example that <u>isn't relevant</u> to the context — e.g. if you're asked why an NGB provides tournaments for beginners, don't waffle on about how they benefit elite performers.

Technology in Sport

1   Draw lines to match **four** roles of technology to the correct practical example.

Role of technology		Practical example
To increase the safety of participants.		A hockey player wears a mouthguard.
To enhance performance.		A laser measures the distance of a discus throw.
To increase accuracy of officiating.		A sports coach cycles to their local leisure centre.
To enhance spectatorship.		A carbon fibre tennis racket giving a player more control of the ball.
		A football stadium has a large screen to show replays to fans.

[4]

2   Describe **two** positive effects of technology on the spectator experience.

1. ....

   ....

2. ....

   ....

[2]

3   Identify **one** example of technology that can be used during training.
Explain **one** negative effect of this technology in sport.

Example of technology:

....

How it can have a negative effect:

....

....

[2]

Technology in Sport

4 Explain how performers have benefitted from improvements
to **two** named examples of sporting equipment.

1. ....

....

2. ....

....

[4]

5 Describe **two** negative effects of technology on sports officials.

1. ....

....

2. ....

....

[2]

Innovations in technology have led to improvements in sports clothing and footwear.

6 (a) Describe **two** examples of clothing or footwear that helps improve performance.

1. ....

....

2. ....

....

[2]

(b) Explain **one** drawback of the development of new clothing or footwear technology in sport.

....

....

....

....

[2]

Exam Tip

There is lots of debate on how much technology should be allowed in sport... it's a perfect topic for an exam question.
Make sure you can recall loads of pros and cons of technology in sport (for performers, spectators and officials).

Short & Medium-Answer Questions — Topic Area 5

Technology in Sport

7 Describe **two** negative effects of technology on spectators.
For each effect, give a practical example.

Effect 1: ....

Practical example: ....

....

Effect 2: ....

Practical example: ....

....

[4]

Boccia is an inclusive sport with many performers using assistive technology.

8 Other than boccia, explain how **one** piece of assistive technology is used in a named sport.

Sport: ....

Explanation: ....

....

....

[2]

9 Identify **three** examples of technology used by officials to support decision making.
Describe how each technology is used in a named sport.

Technology 1: ....

How it is used: ....

....

Technology 2: ....

How it used: ....

....

Technology 3: ....

How it is used: ....

....

[6]

8-Mark Questions — Mark Scheme

The final question in the exam is an extended-response question worth 8 marks.
'**Discuss**...', '**Evaluate**...' and '**Analyse**...' are common command words for this question.

This mark scheme is used for 8-mark questions

This table shows you what examiners are looking for when they mark 8-mark questions.

Number of marks	What's written	How it's written
7-8 marks	The answer shows detailed knowledge and understanding with developed points, supported with examples. There is a justified conclusion (if required).	The answer has excellent structure and shows logical reasoning throughout. The correct terminology is used.
4-6 marks	The answer shows some good knowledge and understanding, with some developed points and examples.	The answer has good structure and shows some logical reasoning throughout. Some appropriate terminology is used.
1-3 marks	The answer shows only limited knowledge and understanding, with few points made and limited or no examples.	The answer has poor structure, and points made are unbalanced. Limited or no terminology is used.
0 marks	There is no relevant information.	There is no relevant information.

To achieve the **top marks**, you'll need to write **well-structured** paragraphs.
You can do this by structuring points in this way:

- Knowledge point (**K**) – make a point to demonstrate your knowledge.
- Development (**D**) – describe and develop your point in more detail.
- Example (**EG**) – give a sporting example to further support your point.

Here's an example of an 8-mark 'Discuss...' question

Performance Enhancing Drugs (PEDs) are used by some professional athletes.

1   Discuss the reasons why PEDs are used by some professional athletes.
You should include:

- Reasons why a professional athlete may take PEDs.

- Reasons why a professional athlete should not take PEDs.

- A justification as to whether PEDs should be allowed in sport.

There are some sample answers to this question on the next page.

[8]

Answering 8-Mark Questions

Read through Answer 1, then look at the explanation of **how many marks** it would get and **why**.
Compare this to the **mark scheme** and the **example points** on the previous page.

Answer 1

Athletes might take PEDs to perform better. It can also help them to be faster or stronger.

The bad thing about performance enhancing drugs is that they can damage an athlete's

health and it is cheating.

This answer gets _2_ mark(s) out of 8, because *it shows some knowledge of PEDs, but there are only basic points. These points have not been developed and there are no sporting examples given.*

Now it's your turn to be the examiner. Read Answer 2 below, then work out which description
from the mark scheme fits this sample answer best to find the mark you think it deserves.

Answer 2

Athletes take PEDs for many reasons, despite the side effects. An athlete may use PEDs to make

themselves stronger and faster, which can help them to perform better in races and win medals.

Dwain Chambers, a British 100m sprinter, used PEDs for this reason but was caught and banned

for a number of years. This had a negative impact on his sporting reputation.

How many marks would **you** give this answer?
Explain **why** you've decided on this mark in the grey box below.

I would give this answer ...... mark(s) out of 8, because

Compare what you've written to the explanation on p.72.

Answering 8-Mark Questions

Now have a go at improving Answer 2 from the previous page so it would get **8 marks**.
Write your answer in the space below, then compare it to the sample answer on p.72.

> Performance Enhancing Drugs (PEDs) are used by some professional athletes.

1 Discuss the reasons why PEDs are used by some professional athletes.

Make sure to cover the bullet points from p.37.

[8]

Don't worry if your answer wouldn't have got 8 marks — the next section gives you lots more practice at these sorts of question.

Top tips for answering 8-mark questions

1 Plan your answer first.
Don't just start writing — take some time to think and plan out your answer.

2 Use the context.
Each point you make should be relevant to the question. Also include everything the bullet points ask for.

3 Structure your paragraphs.
See p.37 — write a knowledge point, develop it and include a relevant sporting example.

4 Write in full sentences.
You get marks for a well-developed argument, so don't write things in note form.

5 Form a conclusion.
Finish off with a conclusion (if relevant), supported by the points you've provided.

Mixed Questions 1

Jas is 15 years old. She has moved from a city to a village in a different part of the UK.
She took part in figure skating sessions at a local ice rink in the city.
The nearest ice rink to her new village is 25 miles away.

1   (a)   Explain **three** barriers to participation that may prevent Jas
from continuing to participate in figure skating.

Barrier 1: ....

Explanation: ....

....

Barrier 2: ....

Explanation: ....

....

Barrier 3: ....

Explanation: ....

....
[6]

(b)   Identify **two** actions that the nearest ice rink could take
to overcome the barriers to participation faced by Jas.

1. ....

....

2. ....

....
[2]

2   Explain, using an example, what a sporting initiative is.

....

....

....

....
[2]

Mixed Questions 1

The table below shows the approximate number of adult participants for a number of sports in the UK in one year.

Sport	Number of participants
Cricket	350 000
Lacrosse	24 000
Netball	290 000
Tennis	900 000
Ultimate frisbee	60 000

3 (a) Identify the sport in the table which has the greatest number of participants. Describe **three** possible reasons why this sport is popular in the UK.

Sport: ....

Reason 1: ....

....

Reason 2: ....

....

Reason 3: ....

....

[4]

(b) Describe **two** possible reasons why netball has a lower number of participants than the sport you identified in part (a).

1. ....

....

2. ....

....

[2]

(c) Ultimate frisbee is an example of an emerging sport in the UK.

Explain how you would expect the number of participants in ultimate frisbee to change in future years.

....

....

[2]

Exam Tip

For Q3, you just need to find the largest number from a set of data. Exam questions could be a bit more involved and ask you to spot trends in data — e.g. comparing participation rates to see if they have increased or decreased over time.

Mixed Questions 1

4 (a) Explain **two** examples of technology that can be used to measure a performer's fitness.

1. ....

....

....

2. ....

....

....

[4]

(b) Other than improving performance, identify **two** roles of technology in sport.
Give a practical example for each role.

Role 1: ....

Practical example: ....

....

Role 2: ....

Practical example: ....

....

[4]

5 (a) Identify **one** NGB and give **one** competition or tournament it organises.

....

....

[2]

(b) State **two** reasons why an NGB may change the rules of a sport.
For each, give a practical example.

Reason 1: ....

Practical example: ....

....

Reason 2: ....

Practical example: ....

....

[4]

Mixed Questions 1

Bidding to host a major sporting event, such as the FIFA World Cup™, is a very lengthy process.

6 Discuss the possible reasons why a country may bid to host a major sporting event.

You should include:

- Positive effects of bidding on the host country.

- Negative effects of bidding on the host country.

- An evaluation of whether the positive effects outweigh the negative effects.

Remember to include real-life examples to support your answer.

[8]

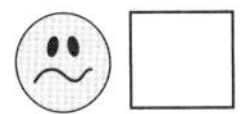  

Mixed Questions 2

1   (a)   Describe what National Governing Bodies (NGBs) are.

....

....
[1]

(b)   State the names of **two** NGBs in the UK.

1. ....

2. ....
[2]

(c)   Identify **three** key roles of an NGB.

1. ....

2. ....

3. ....
[3]

Performers are at risk of injury when they participate in sport.

2   (a)   Using sporting examples, explain **two** types of equipment
that can help to protect performers from injury.

1. ....

....

....

2. ....

....

....
[4]

(b)   Describe **one** type of technology that can help
a performer recover more quickly from an injury.

....

....

....

....
[2]

Mixed Questions 2

It is important that performers follow the etiquette of a sport.

3 (a) Describe what is meant by the term sporting etiquette and give **two** reasons why it is important for performers to demonstrate good sporting etiquette.

Description: ....

....

Reason 1: ....

....

Reason 2: ....

....

[3]

(b) Describe **two** practical examples of performers demonstrating sporting etiquette.

1. ....

....

2. ....

....

[2]

4 (a) Identify whether the following major sporting events are regular, one-off or regular and recurring events.

Olympic Games: ....

British Grand Prix: ....

[2]

(b) Other than the sporting events in part (a), give an example of a major sporting event and explain what type of event it is.

Major sporting event: ....

Type of event: ....

....

[2]

Exam Tip

Watch out — there's <u>sporting</u> etiquette (shown by performers) and <u>spectator</u> etiquette (yep, shown by spectators). It goes without saying, really — make sure you write about the correct one in the question or you won't get the marks.

Mixed Questions 2

Footgolf can be described as an emerging sport in the UK.

5 (a) Describe what is meant by the term 'emerging sport'.

....

....

[1]

(b) Other than footgolf, state **two** emerging sports in the UK.

1. ....

2. ....

[2]

(c) Identify **two** factors that impact the popularity of footgolf in the UK.

1. ....

....

2. ....

....

[2]

The World Anti-Doping Agency (WADA) was created to try to stop drug use in sport.

6 (a) Describe the whereabouts rule used by WADA.

....

....

....

....

[2]

(b) Other than the whereabouts rule, describe **two** methods
that WADA uses to reduce drug use in sport.

1. ....

....

2. ....

....

[2]

Mixed Questions 2

Media coverage of a sport can impact its popularity.

7   Discuss the impact of media coverage on the popularity of a sport.

You should include:

- The amount and range of media coverage that is available.

- How media coverage can increase a sport's popularity.

- An evaluation of the extent to which a sport's popularity relies on media coverage.

[8]

Mixed Questions 3

The Olympic Games has a symbol, a creed and three values.

1   (a)   State whether the Olympic symbol, the creed or the values are being described below.

A message for athletes that it is important to try your best, not just win.

....

Five interlocking rings representing the closeness of the five continents.

....

[2]

(b)   Other than friendship, explain **one** Olympic value and give a practical example of it.

Value: ....

Explanation: ....

....

Practical example: ....

....

[3]

People sometimes object to hosting a major sporting event for financial reasons.

2   (a)   Describe **two** financial objections people may have
to their city hosting a major sporting event.

1. ....

....

2. ....

....

[2]

(b)   Describe **two** financial benefits to a city of hosting a major sporting event.

1. ....

....

2. ....

....

[2]

Mixed Questions 3

Donna is a single parent with a 2-year-old son. She is unemployed and does not own a car. The leisure centre five miles from her home is offering free taster sessions for some sports.

	Padel — taster session	Walking football — taster session
Mon-Fri	9 – 10 am	1 – 2 pm
Sat-Sun	10 – 11 am	*No sessions*

3   (a)   Explain **two** barriers that could prevent Donna from taking part in one of the taster sessions.

Barrier 1: ....

Explanation: ....

....

Barrier 2: ....

Explanation: ....

....
[4]

(b)   Describe **one** solution to a barrier you identified in part (a).

....

....
[1]

(c)   Padel and walking football can both be described as emerging sports.

Other than offering taster sessions, identify **two** ways of increasing participation in emerging sports.

1. ....

....

2. ....

....
[2]

Exam Tip

Many factors can prevent people from taking part in physical activity — e.g. age, disabilities... but they don't apply to everyone. In exam questions, you must always refer to the barriers that are specific to the participant.

Mixed Questions 3

Many fans choose to watch live sporting events in person.

4 (a) Identify **two** ways that technology could impact their experience.

1. ....

....

2. ....

....

[2]

(b) Identify **two** ways that fans might use technology to access sports coverage.
State **one** advantage of accessing sports coverage in each way.
Give a different advantage for each.

Way 1: ....

Advantage: ....

....

Way 2: ....

Advantage: ....

....

[4]

5 (a) Identify the organisation that aims to eradicate the use of PEDs in sport worldwide.

....

[1]

(b) Describe **two** approaches used to prevent performers using PEDs.

1. ....

....

2. ....

....

[2]

Mixed Questions 3

A National Governing Body (NGB) manages a specific sport within a country.

6   Discuss, using examples, the following statement:

'The most important function of an NGB is to promote participation in their sport.'

You should include:

* The different ways NGBs aim to increase participation in their sport.

* The other functions of NGBs.

* A justification of your view about whether the statement is true or not.

....

....

....

....

....

....

....

....

....

....

....

....

....

....

....

....

[8]

Exam Tip

Make sure you use the appropriate terminology in your answers, or you're at risk of losing some easy marks.
E.g. 'promote participation', rather than 'try to get more players', and 'lobby for funding', rather than 'ask for dosh'.

Mixed Questions 4

Billy is 16 years old. He regularly has to care for his dad before and after college.

1   (a)   State **two** user groups that Billy belongs to.

1. ....

2. ....

[2]

(b)   Billy loves to take part in sport with his friends but often isn't able to do so.
Identify **three** possible barriers which could prevent him from participating in sport.

1. ....

2. ....

3. ....

[3]

(c)   Describe **three** possible solutions that would help Billy participate in sport.

1. ....

....

2. ....

....

3. ....

....

[3]

One role of technology is to enhance performance. For example,
improvements to golf clubs allow players to hit the ball further.

2   Other than sports equipment, identify **two** types of technology that enhance performance.
For each type, give a specific example.

Type 1: ....

....

Example: ....

Type 2: ....

....

Example: ....

[4]

Mixed Questions 4

3   Describe **two** types of major sporting events, giving an example of each.

1. ....

....

....

2. ....

....

....

[4]

A goal for many athletes is to compete at the Olympic or Paralympic Games.
Athletes are expected to follow a set of values when competing in these sporting events.

4   (a)   Describe how the following values are promoted through
participation in the Paralympic Games.

Inspiration

....

....

Determination

....

....

Equality

....

....

[3]

(b)   Identify the **three** Olympic values.

1. ....

2. ....

3. ....

[3]

Section 2 — Mixed Questions

Mixed Questions 4

The decisions of sporting officials are often scrutinised.
Technology is increasingly being used to help with officiating.

5 (a) Identify **two** pieces of technology that an official can use to help with decision making.
For each piece of technology, give a practical example of its use.

Technology 1: ....

Practical example: ....

....

Technology 2: ....

Practical example: ....

....

[4]

(b) Describe **one** potential drawback of using technology to help with officiating.

....

....

[1]

Promoting and developing sport can be expensive for NGBs in the UK.

6 (a) Describe **one** way a named NGB may develop their sport in the UK.

....

....

....

....

[2]

(b) Identify **three** ways that an NGB could gain money to develop their sport in the UK.

1. ....

2. ....

3. ....

[3]

Mixed Questions 4

Some athletes choose to take Performance Enhancing Drugs (PEDs), even though there can be severe consequences of doing so.

7   Discuss the reasons why PEDs are used by athletes.

You should include:

- Reasons why an athlete may choose to take PEDs.

- Reasons why an athlete should not take PEDs.

- An evaluation as to whether taking PEDs can ever be justified.

....

....

....

....

....

....

....

....

....

....

....

....

....

....

....

....

[8]

Mixed Questions 5

Roberta is a first-year university student. She is currently looking for a part-time job.
She enjoyed playing squash when she was younger and would like to begin playing again.

1 (a) Identify **three** barriers that could prevent Roberta from playing squash.

1. ....

2. ....

3. ....
[3]

(b) Explain **two** possible solutions to the barriers you identified in part (a).

Solution 1: ....

....

Solution 2: ....

....
[4]

2 (a) Describe what is meant by demonstrating good spectator etiquette.

....

....
[1]

(b) State **three** examples of good spectator etiquette.

1. ....

....

2. ....

....

3. ....

....
[3]

Mixed Questions 5

3   (a)   State the **three** levels at which sporting initiatives can take place.

1. ....

2. ....

3. ....

[3]

     (b)   Identify **one** sporting initiative and describe its aim.

Sporting initiative: ....

Aim: ....

....

[2]

4   Hosting a major sporting event has benefits and drawbacks.

     (a)   State **three** benefits that a host city is likely to experience **during** the sporting event.

1. ....

....

2. ....

....

3. ....

....

[3]

     (b)   A host city is also likely to encounter problems **during** the sporting event.
Identify **two** of these problems.

1. ....

....

2. ....

....

[2]

Exam Tip

Question 4 shows why you must read the question carefully. You need to give two problems that may occur during the event (yup, it is even bolded). If you give pre-event or post-event problems you won't get the marks.

Mixed Questions 5

5   (a)   State **two** reasons why an athlete might decide to take performance enhancing drugs.

1. ....

....

2. ....

....

[2]

    (b)   State **three** reasons why athletes should **not** take performance enhancing drugs.

1. ....

....

2. ....

....

3. ....

....

[3]

Football is a very popular sport in the UK. One reason for this is that there are a large number of opportunities to spectate football matches.

6   Explain **two** other factors that are likely to contribute to football's popularity in the UK.

Factor 1: ....

Explanation: ....

....

....

Factor 2: ....

Explanation: ....

....

....

[4]

Mixed Questions 5

Technology now plays a vital role in most sports at the elite level.

7   Discuss the impacts of technology in elite level sport.

You should include:

- Positive impacts on sport at the elite level.

- Negative impacts on sport at the elite level.

- A justification of whether technology in sport has an overall positive or negative impact at the elite level.

....

....

....

....

....

....

....

....

....

....

....

....

....

....

....

[8]

Exam Tip

Those 8-mark questions can look pretty scary... but they're also a source of easy marks if you know what you're doing. You'll usually need to consider things from two angles, then come to some sort of justified conclusion.

Mixed Questions 6

Ronnie is a 35-year-old single father. He has a low fitness level and would like to improve it. However, he has young children who he must take care of, except when they are at school.

The table below shows the timetable of activities at a local sports facility.

Day	6 am to 7 am	10 am to 11 am	2 pm to 3 pm	7 pm to 8 pm
Monday	Circuits			Aqua aerobics
Tuesday		High-intensity circuits	High-intensity aerobics	
Wednesday				Low-intensity circuits
Thursday	Low-intensity circuits	High-intensity aerobics		
Friday				High-intensity circuits
Saturday	Circuits	High-intensity body pump	High-intensity aerobics	
Sunday	High-intensity aerobics			Low-intensity circuits

1 (a) Using the information provided, explain **one** barrier to participation faced by Ronnie.

....

....

....

[2]

(b) Describe **two** ways that the sports facility could help Ronnie participate.

1. ....

....

2. ....

....

[2]

(c) Explain how **one** solution you identified in part (b) would impact the sports facility.

....

....

[1]

Mixed Questions 6

Two important roles of National Governing Bodies (NGB) are ensuring the safety of participants and providing support to members.

2 (a) Identify **two** ways that an NGB can help to create a safe environment for its participants.

1. ....

2. ....

[2]

(b) State **three** ways an NGB can support their members.

1. ....

2. ....

3. ....

[3]

3 (a) Explain what sportsmanship is and give **two** sporting examples.

Explanation: ....

....

Example 1: ....

....

Example 2: ....

....

[3]

(b) Explain what gamesmanship is and give **two** sporting examples.

Explanation: ....

....

Example 1: ....

....

Example 2: ....

....

[3]

Exam Tip

Try not to be vague in your answers, especially with questions where you need to 'Explain' something. It's always a good idea to be as specific as you can, with clear and relevant answers to back up the point you're making.

Mixed Questions 6

4 (a) Using an example, describe what is meant by an **international** sporting event.

....

....

....
[2]

(b) State the **three** ways that a major sporting event can be scheduled.

1. ....

2. ....

3. ....
[3]

Rugby union referees wear microphones for televised games so that spectators can hear what they say during the game.

5 (a) Describe **two** positive impacts of this use of technology.

1. ....

....

2. ....

....
[2]

(b) Describe **two other** ways that technology has enhanced spectatorship.
For each way, give an example.

Way 1: ....

....

Example: ....

Way 2: ....

....

Example: ....
[4]

Mixed Questions 6

A major sporting event, such as the Olympic Games, can continue
to impact the host city or country for many years after the event.

6 Evaluate the post-event impacts of hosting a major sporting event.

You should include:

- Positive post-event impacts of hosting.

- Negative post-event impacts of hosting.

- An evaluation of whether the positive impacts outweigh the negative impacts.

....

....

....

....

....

....

....

....

....

....

....

....

....

....

....

....

[8]

Exam Tip

Answers to many exam questions (e.g. 'Explain' or 'Evaluate' questions) should be written in full sentences — don't go
writing in note form or bullets. With questions like the one above, you'll be expected to link your points together.

Section 2 — Mixed Questions

Mixed Questions 7

John is a 10-year-old boy who wants to become involved in a team game.
The table below shows information about the four clubs nearest to John's home.

Sport	Distance from John's home	Cost per session	Day and time	Own equipment needed?
Basketball	15 miles	Free	Saturday (4 pm)	No
Rugby union	2 miles	£8	Saturday (10 am)	Yes — mouthguard
Handball	2 miles	£3	Tuesday (2 pm)	No
Lacrosse	0.5 miles	£2	Monday (4.45 pm)	Yes — lacrosse stick

1   (a)   Using the information in the table, describe **one** barrier
that might prevent John from taking part in each sport.

Basketball: ....

....

Rugby union: ....

....

Handball: ....

....

Lacrosse: ....

....

[4]

(b)   Identify **three** solutions the clubs could offer to help John take part in their sport.

1. ....

....

2. ....

....

3. ....

....

[3]

Mixed Questions 7

2 Using examples, explain **two** possible consequences of
poor spectator etiquette during live sporting performances.

1. ....

....

....

2. ....

....

....

[4]

Major sporting events, such as the Olympic Games, usually take place in one particular city.

3 Describe **one positive** and **one negative** aspect of the increased number
of visitors during a sporting event for people who live in the host city.

Positive aspect: ....

....

....

Negative aspect: ....

....

....

[2]

4 Describe **two** actions a local swimming pool could take to make their
facilities more accessible for people with disabilities.

1. ....

....

2. ....

....

[2]

Exam Tip

Written something a bit stupid that you don't want the examiner to mark? Don't fret — simply draw a neat,
straight line through it (a bit like this: ~~Ollymicpicks~~) to show that it is something that you don't want marking.

  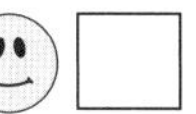 

Mixed Questions 7

British Swimming is an NGB which promotes participation in water polo.

5 (a) Identify **one** other NGB and name a sport it is responsible for promoting.

NGB: ....

Sport: ....

[2]

(b) Describe **two** ways that the NGB you have named could promote participation in their sport.

1. ....

....

2. ....

....

[2]

(c) Using an example, explain how an NGB can develop their sport's coaching infrastructure.

....

....

....

[2]

Technology has many impacts on sport and on performers.

6 (a) Identify **one** positive impact and **one** negative impact of technology on fair play in sport.

Positive impact: ....

....

Negative impact: ....

....

[2]

(b) State **one** example of technology used for injury recovery.
Describe how it helps a performer to recover from an injury.

....

....

....

[2]

Mixed Questions 7

The barriers to participation in sport faced by teenagers are different to those faced by adults.

7   Compare and contrast the barriers to participation faced
     by a typical teenager with those faced by an adult.

     You should include:

     • Barriers to participation commonly faced by teenagers.

     • Barriers to participation commonly faced by adults.

     • A justification of your view as to whether the barriers faced by
       teenagers or by adults are generally more challenging to overcome.

....

....

....

....

....

....

....

....

....

....

....

....

....

....

....

....

[8]

Exam Tip

When you're answering an 8-mark question, stay focused on what the question is asking and don't go off on a tangent.
For example, in the question above, don't write about the barriers faced by young children just to fill a bit of space.

Section 2 — Mixed Questions

Answers

Exam Skills 1

Page 5: Answering Short & Medium-Answer Questions

I would give this answer 1 mark(s) out of 4, because courage is not a sporting value, but a Paralympic value, so this cannot receive any marks. Citizenship is a sporting value that has been explained correctly. However, the example doesn't mention a specific sport.

Here's an example of an improved answer for the 4-mark question:
Value 1: National pride is showing support for your national team.
Sporting example: Singing your country's national anthem when spectating a FIFA World Cup™ football match.
Value 2: Citizenship is about creating links in the local community.
Sporting example: A kayaker volunteering at a beginners' session at their local swimming pool.
You could have also explained team spirit, fair play or tolerance and respect.

Short & Medium-Answer Questions — Topic Area 1

Pages 6-7: User Groups

1   Retired people — People who no longer work and may receive money from a pension.
Carers — Adults or children who care for family members.
Economically disadvantaged people — People who have a lack of disposable income.
Parents — A single person or couple raising children.
[4 marks available — 1 mark for each correct match]

2   Some people in this user group have a disability that is not visible.
[1 mark]

3   Any three from: people with family commitments / parents / families with children / carers.
[3 marks available — 1 mark for each user group]

4   Parents *[1 mark]*

5   E.g.
User group 1: Parents *[1 mark]*
Explanation: It is easier for them to participate in sport while their children are in school. *[1 mark]*
User group 2: People over 60 *[1 mark]*
Explanation: They may be less likely to drive, so may find it easier to participate during the daytime when public transport is more frequent. *[1 mark]*
There are lots of user groups you could name here — any answer is fine with a sensible explanation.

6   (a) Any one from: young children / teenagers / people over 60.
[1 mark]
    (b) E.g. young children may need:
activities that are not during school time / activities with a fun or social element / activities that are not expensive.
[2 marks available — 1 mark for each need]

Pages 8-11: Barriers to Participation

1   Lack of disposable income — Introduce discounts for unemployed people who may struggle to afford fees.
Lack of awareness of appropriate activity provision — Advertise activities for teenagers on social media where teenagers are likely to see these adverts.
Lack of positive sporting role models from minority ethnic groups — Increase the diversity of coaches and sports leaders.
[3 marks available — 1 mark for each correct match]

2   E.g. if a young child has a lack of positive family support/role models, they are unlikely to be encouraged to participate in sport.
[2 marks available — 1 mark for a barrier to participation, 1 mark for a linked explanation]

3   Provide sessions at a range of times. *[1 mark]*

4   E.g.
Lack of equal coverage of different genders by the media
Explanation: There is an imbalance of media coverage of men's and women's sports. *[1 mark]*
Practical example: There is greater TV coverage of men's football than women's football. *[1 mark]*
Lack of family support
Explanation: If a family has a negative attitude towards sport, it may discourage a child from taking part. *[1 mark]*
Practical example: A child would like to try judo. Their parents think sport isn't important and won't take them, so they don't take part. *[1 mark]*
Family commitments
Explanation: Someone responsible for looking after/helping a family member may not have time to participate in sport. *[1 mark]*
Practical example: A single mother can't go swimming because she has to take care of her young children. *[1 mark]*

5   (a) E.g. install ramps so they can access all parts of the facility.
[1 mark]
    (b) E.g. provide Braille signage so they can find their way around. *[1 mark]*
    (c) E.g. install hearing loops in key areas. *[1 mark]*

6   (a) E.g.
User group: People with disabilities
Explanation: Not all public transport is easily accessible for people with physical impairments.
[2 marks available — 1 mark for a user group, 1 mark for a linked explanation]
    (b) E.g. ramps should be provided for wheelchair users at train stations so they can access trains and platforms. *[1 mark]*

7   E.g. the media may neglect to cover athletes from ethnic minority groups, so there may be fewer role models for people from these user groups / the media may use images to promote a sport that reinforces stereotypes, e.g. only using white athletes for golf events.
[2 marks available — 1 mark for each way]

8   E.g.
Barrier: Lack of activity provision
Solution: A wide range of sports sessions should be made available — low-intensity classes would be more suitable for an older person.
[2 marks available — 1 mark for a barrier, 1 mark for a linked solution]
Other possible barriers include a lack of disposable income, a lack of transport and a lack of positive sporting role models.

9   (a) Any three from: e.g. use targeted advertisements / promote role models / use sporting initiatives / offer incentives such as taster sessions.
[3 marks available — 1 mark for each strategy]
    (b) Targeted promotion is advertising or special offers that are aimed at a specific user group. *[1 mark]*
    (c) E.g. teenagers may have a lack of awareness of activity provision. Advertising on social media could be a solution to this barrier as teenagers are likely to see an advert on social media.
[2 marks available — 1 mark for a user group, 1 mark for a solution to a barrier]

10 (a) E.g. unemployed people may not have enough disposable income to pay participation fees. *[1 mark]*
    (b) E.g. offer reduced prices of activities for people who are unemployed or on low incomes. *[1 mark]*

Answers

Pages 12-14: Popularity of Sport

1   There are few opportunities to watch the sport being performed. *[1 mark]*

2   E.g.
Factor 1: The number of people participating.
Explanation: Events like the London Marathon have lots of participants and media attention, which increases the number of other people wanting to take part in running.
Factor 2: The provision of facilities.
Explanation: There are many local leisure centres with swimming pools in the UK, so there are many opportunities for people to take part in swimming classes.
Factor 3: The environment.
Explanation: The UK has a lot of coastline, so there are lots of opportunities to take part in water sports like sailing.
Factor 4: The number of live spectator opportunities.
Explanation: Many subscription packages allow spectators to watch live Premier League games at home, which increases the popularity of football.
[8 marks available — 1 mark for each factor, 1 mark for a linked explanation with a sporting example]

3   E.g.
Sport: Rowing
Explanation: The UK has many lakes and rivers, so rowing is accessible and therefore popular.
[2 marks available — 1 mark for a suitable sport, 1 mark for a linked explanation]

4   Any three from: e.g. more media coverage of a sport will make more people aware of the sport / media coverage can promote role models who inspire people to take part in the sport / the media provides analysis of a sport which helps people feel more involved in the sport / pundits can educate people about a sport so they understand and enjoy the sport more.
[3 marks available — 1 mark for each reason]

5   E.g. After the England football team won the UEFA Women's EURO in 2022, the popularity of women's football increased. / After Team GB's cycling success in the 2012 Olympics, the popularity of cycling increased.
[2 marks available — 1 mark for each example]

6   (a) E.g. Emma Raducanu inspired girls to take up tennis after becoming the first British female winner at the US Open since 1968, at the age of 18.
[2 marks available — 1 mark for a role model, 1 mark for a linked explanation]

     (b) E.g. it is important to inspire people from all user groups to participate in sport. *[1 mark]*
You could also reference the sporting value of 'inclusion' here too.

7   E.g. Olympic sports receive lots of media coverage which may introduce new people to the sport / Olympic athletes from the sport may be seen as role models.
[2 marks available — 1 mark for each reason]

8   E.g.
Reason 1: It is considered to be violent.
Sporting example: People punch each other in boxing, so some people consider it to be a violent sport.
Reason 2: It is cruel to animals.
Sporting example: Horse racing may be considered cruel as some horses get injured and may have to be put down as a result.
[4 marks available — 1 mark for each reason, 1 mark for a linked explanation]

Page 15: Emerging and New Sports in the UK

1   An emerging sport is a sport which is significantly gaining popularity in a country. *[1 mark]*

2   E.g.
Emerging sport: korfball *[1 mark]*
Reason 1: It can be played in mixed teams, so it is inclusive of different genders. *[1 mark]*
Reason 2: It uses skills from traditional sports such as basketball and netball. *[1 mark]*

3   E.g.
Action 1: Train more coaches and officials.
Explanation: There will be more opportunities for people to be involved in the sport.
Action 2: Run advertising campaigns.
Explanation: There will be an increased awareness of the sport.
Action 3: Change the rules.
Explanation: Rule changes can make a sport more exciting, which can encourage more people to take part or spectate.
[6 marks available — 1 mark for each action, 1 mark for each linked explanation]

Short & Medium-Answer Questions — Topic Area 2

Pages 16-17: Sporting Values

1   Tolerance and respect — Developing an understanding of other cultures.
Citizenship — Creating community links and spirit through involvement in local sports clubs and teams.
Inclusion — Equal opportunities for all social groups to participate in sport.
National pride — The unity of the whole population in support of the country's team or squad.
[4 marks available — 1 mark for each match]

2   Any two from: e.g. adapting a sport so that people with disabilities can participate / developing initiatives to increase participation of minority groups / volunteers offering to train economically disadvantaged people.
[2 marks available — 1 mark for each example]

3   Wearing Rainbow Laces to show support of LGBTQ+ people in sport. *[1 mark]*

4   E.g.
Fair play — owning up to a foot fault when serving in badminton. *[1 mark]*
Team spirit — not making a teammate feel bad if they miss a penalty in football. *[1 mark]*
Excellence — a gymnast attending all training sessions and trying their best. *[1 mark]*
Tolerance and respect — a sports team bowing to spectators when playing in Japan. *[1 mark]*

5   (a) E.g. joining with other people in fan parks to support the national team in the FIFA World Cup™. *[1 mark]*

     (b) E.g. remaining quiet through the opposition team's national anthem. *[1 mark]*

Pages 18-19: The Olympic and Paralympic Movement

1   Equality, courage, inspiration and determination. *[1 mark]*

2   E.g. The Olympic creed is a moral message *[1 mark]* which says that it is more important to take part than to win *[1 mark]*.

3   (a) The symbol is made of five interlocking rings. *[1 mark]*

     (b) E.g. each ring represents one of the five continents that take part in the Olympic Games *[1 mark]*. The interlocking nature represents the closeness/unity of the continents *[1 mark]*.

     (c) E.g. the Olympic Games involves performers and spectators from all over the world *[1 mark]*, so friendship is important to encourage understanding between different people *[1 mark]*.

Answers

4   E.g.
Way 1: They respect the rules of the sport. *[1 mark]*
Practical example: A table tennis player does not try
to perform illegal serves in a match. *[1 mark]*
Way 2: They respect their body. *[1 mark]*
Practical example: A sprinter not taking PEDs,
as they can damage health. *[1 mark]*

5   Courage *[1 mark]*
Determination *[1 mark]*
Equality *[1 mark]*

Page 20: Sporting Initiatives

1   It usually has access to large amounts of funding. *[1 mark]*

2   E.g.
Fair play
Sporting initiative: FA Respect
Example: It encourages performers to respect
referees and the decisions they make.
Inclusion
Sporting initiative: Rainbow Laces
Example: It encourages performers to wear rainbow
laces to raise awareness of the discrimination that
the LGBTQ+ community face in sport.
*[4 marks available — 1 mark for each initiative,
1 mark for each example]*

3   (a) E.g.
Initiative: THIS GIRL CAN *[1 mark]*
Target group: women and girls *[1 mark]*
     (b) E.g. It is a national initiative because it runs
across the whole country. *[1 mark]*
*A regional initiative runs across part of the UK, e.g.
Stronger 4 Longer is a regional initiative in Somerset.*

Pages 21-23: Sporting Behaviour

1   Showing good sportsmanship upholds the spirit of the game.
[1 mark]

2   It does not involve breaking the rules of the sport. *[1 mark]*

3   Sportsmanship — A tennis player owning up if they return a ball
after a double bounce.
Gamesmanship — A footballer time-wasting before a goal kick.
Spectator etiquette — Fans applauding skilful performances
of both teams.
[3 marks available — 1 mark for each match]

4   Breaking the flow of the game: e.g. football players may
exaggerate an injury to cause a long break in play. *[1 mark]*
Distracting opponents: e.g. tennis players sometimes grunt
when they hit the ball to distract their opponent. *[1 mark]*

5   E.g.
Reason 1: To create a good atmosphere.
Practical example: Spectators applauding when a batter in
cricket hits the ball over the boundary line for six runs.
Reason 2: To show respect towards others.
Practical example: Football spectators at the FIFA World Cup™
not booing the national anthem of the other team.
Reason 3: To keep performers safe.
Practical example: Spectators keeping quiet at a show jumping
event, so the horses stay calm and don't throw off their riders.
*[6 marks available — 1 mark for each reason,
1 mark for each linked example]*

6   (a) E.g. sportsmanship is following the rules of the sport
[1 mark] and treating other people with respect *[1 mark]*.
     (b) E.g.
Team spirit: a batter in cricket supporting their partner when
they are immediately bowled out. *[1 mark]*

Fair play: a footballer respecting the decision of a referee to
give a free kick. *[1 mark]*

7   (a) E.g. a hockey player raising a hockey stick above the shoulder
would endanger other players / a rugby player performing a
high tackle would likely injure the attacking player.
[2 marks available — 1 mark for each example]
     (b) E.g. shouting during a gymnast's routine could make
them lose concentration and fall and injure themselves
/ invading a football pitch after the final whistle
can lead to violence towards opposing players.
[2 marks available — 1 mark for each example]

Pages 24-25: Performance Enhancing Drugs

1   To improve their overall health. *[1 mark]*

2   Any two from: e.g. performers can be banned from competing
/ PEDs can damage health and lead to addiction / PEDs
can mask injuries, leading to greater damage / PEDs can
harm the performer's reputation if they are caught.
Any two from: e.g. PEDs can undermine the spirit of the sport
and the values it should represent / PEDs cause spectators
to distrust results of sporting events / PEDs can stop people
participating in sport if they think other competitors will be
using them / PEDs can reduce the number of role models,
meaning fewer people are inspired to participate.
[4 marks available — 1 mark for each impact]

3   (a) E.g. WADA's Play True Day *[1 mark]*
     (b) Role models are admired by many people *[1 mark]*,
so people are more likely to be influenced by the
message/take notice of the strategy *[1 mark]*.

4   (a) World Anti-Doping Agency *[1 mark]*
     (b) Drug testing *[1 mark]*, developing anti-doping policies
[1 mark]

5   Performers can only be tested during competitions. *[1 mark]*
Performers may be tested on any date and anywhere.

6   E.g.
Sanction 1: Ban from the sport
Example: Simona Halep (tennis player) was
given a four year ban for doping violations.
Sanction 2: Fine
Example: Lance Armstrong (cyclist) had to repay
his winnings from the Tour de France.
*[4 marks available — 1 mark for each sanction,
1 mark for each linked example]*

Short & Medium-Answer Questions — Topic Area 3

Page 26: Types of Sporting Event

1   Winter Paralympic Games — One-off event
UEFA Champions League Final — Regular event
Wimbledon — Regular and recurring event
[3 marks available — 1 mark for each match]

2   One-off event — e.g. the host city is different each time
and a city won't host again for a generation. *[1 mark]*
Regular and recurring event — e.g. the event happens
at the same host city each year. *[1 mark]*

3   E.g. A regular major sporting event happens each year in a
different city. An example is The OPEN® Championship (golf).
*[2 marks available — 1 mark for a
definition, 1 mark for an example]*

4   An international event involves participants and
spectators from two or more countries. Hundreds of
countries attend the Olympic Games. *[1 mark]*

Answers

Pages 27-30: Hosting Sporting Events

1 Increased traffic and litter *[1 mark]*

2 (a) E.g. Direct tourism is where people visit and spend money in a host country/city during a sporting event. *[1 mark]*

(b) Any one from: e.g. local businesses would receive more money / the city would have increased traffic / the city would have increased litter / the city could be a target for crime and terrorism. *[1 mark]*

3 (a) Any three from: e.g. roads / cycling paths / railways / stadiums / training facilities / hotels.
[3 marks available — 1 mark for each example]

(b) Any two from: e.g. it attracts financial investment to the country / it gives a potential for increased employment / it increases participation and national interest in sport.
[2 marks available — 1 mark for each benefit]

4 Taxes are raised if costs were more than the revenue generated.
[1 mark]

5 Any three from: e.g. bidding is very expensive / there are huge financial risks from a failed bid / the host country must commit to building new infrastructure / there will be objections to spending money on bidding rather than other needs / other areas of the host country may lose out on funding.
[3 marks available — 1 mark for each drawback]

6 Positive impact: e.g. media coverage would make people more aware of the country, leading to more tourism. *[1 mark]*
Negative impact: e.g. media coverage could highlight failures of the host country, lowering global reputation. *[1 mark]*

7 Any two from: e.g. local people can use new sporting facilities / local people can use improved infrastructure / increased participation in sport could contribute to a healthier population / the country will have an improved global reputation / the country may have more financial investment in the future.
[2 marks available — 1 mark for each benefit]

8 Improved infrastructure — London 2012 Olympics: upgrades and new services on the London Underground.
Increased profile of sport — Tokyo 2020 Olympics: skateboarding makes its debut appearance at the Olympics.
Unused sporting facilities — Athens 2004 Olympics: many venues used for Olympic events are now abandoned.
[3 marks available — 1 mark for each match]

9 E.g. Poor home team performances can damage national morale — Australian morale was likely damaged after being knocked out at the group stages of the 2022 ICC T20 World Cup they hosted.
*[2 marks available — 1 mark for an explanation,
1 mark for a linked example]*
Equally, good home team performances boost national morale, e.g. the success of Team GB's cyclists at the London 2012 Olympics.

10 Any two from: e.g. there will be a threat of increased crime and terrorism / there will be traffic congestion during the event / money could be better spent on other social needs / taxes may rise to cover the cost of hosting the event.
[2 marks available — 1 mark for each reason]

11 Positive aspect: e.g. restaurants and hotels close to host venues would receive more trade and money. *[1 mark]*
Negative aspect: e.g. there would be more litter. *[1 mark]*

12 E.g.
Explanation: It can reduce the global reputation of the country, discouraging tourism and investment.
Example: The Russian doping scandal uncovered after the Sochi 2014 Olympics may have put businesses off investing in the country in future.
*[2 marks available — 1 mark for an explanation,
1 mark for a linked example]*

13 E.g.
Benefit 1: Local people benefit from improved infrastructure.
Example: Westfield Stratford City, built next to the London Olympic Park.
Benefit 2: There may be a greater national interest in sport.
Example: The success of the England football team in the 2022 Women's EURO.
Benefit 3: The media may promote successful sporting events, increasing the global reputation of the country.
Example: South Africa's global reputation was improved by hosting the 2010 FIFA World Cup™.
*[6 marks available — 1 mark for each benefit,
1 mark for each linked example]*

Short & Medium-Answer Questions — Topic Area 4

Pages 31-33: National Governing Bodies

1 An organisation that manages a specific sport in a country.
[1 mark]

2 Any two from: e.g. they advertise using the media to make people more aware of the sport / they organise new competitions to expose more people to the sport / they promote diversity and inclusion in their sport to encourage all user groups to participate.
[2 marks available — 1 mark for each way]

3 (a) Any four from: e.g. fundraising events / donations / sponsorship deals / collecting membership fees / merchandise sales / National Lottery grants / Sport England grants.
[4 marks available — 1 mark for each source]

(b) Any three from: e.g. to pay elite performers / to pay staff / to improve facilities / to fund schemes or initiatives / to host competitions.
[3 marks available — 1 mark for each reason]

4 Any three from: e.g. they bring more money and funding into the sport / they attract new people and fans to the sport / they increase the number of participants in the sport / they can improve the diversity within the sport.
[3 marks available — 1 mark for each impact]

5 (a) Any two from: e.g. suspension from competitions for a set period of time / fines / lifetime bans from the sport.
[2 marks available — 1 mark for each measure]

(b) E.g.
Reason: To make the sport more exciting for spectators.
Example: The 'back-pass rule' in football was introduced to stop defenders from time-wasting.
*[2 marks available — 1 mark for a reason,
1 mark for a linked example]*

6 E.g. training for current officials would make sport fairer as rules would be applied more consistently / training new officials would mean more competitions could be organised.
[2 marks available — 1 mark for each reason]

7 E.g.
Type of support 1: Funding — a large tennis club may apply for funding from the LTA Community Tennis Fund to make their facilities more accessible.
Type of support 2: Technical guidance — a new gymnastics club may ask British Gymnastics to advise them on the equipment that the club will need at their venue.
*[4 marks available — 1 mark for each type of
support, 1 mark for each linked explanation]*
*Another type of support you might have
identified here is advice on insurance.*

8 (a) E.g. Go-Ride (British Cycling) *[1 mark]*

(b) E.g. Local Go-Ride clubs offer fun activities to encourage young people to take part in cycling. *[1 mark]*

Answers

9 E.g.
Way 1: Enforce the use of protective equipment.
Example: Boxers must wear boxing gloves when fighting.
Way 2: Adapt the rules to reduce the chance of injury.
Example: The tackle height in rugby union was lowered to improve player safety when tackling.
[4 marks available — 1 mark for each way, 1 mark for each linked example]

Short & Medium-Answer Questions — Topic Area 5

Pages 34-36: Technology in Sport

1 To increase the safety of participants — a hockey player wears a mouthguard.
To enhance performance — a carbon fibre tennis racket giving a player more control of the ball.
To increase accuracy of officiating — a laser measures the distance of a discus throw.
To enhance spectatorship — a football stadium has a large screen to show replays to fans.
[4 marks available — 1 mark for each match]

2 Any two from: e.g. fans can pause and replay live TV so can't miss key events / statistics during live games keep fans engaged and informed / stadiums have large screens for fans to view appeals / social media allows fans to engage with other fans or performers.
[2 marks available — 1 mark for each positive effect]

3 E.g.
Example of technology: GPS vests
How it can have a negative effect: GPS vests are expensive, so teams that can afford them are at an advantage over teams that can't afford them.
[2 marks available — 1 mark for a technology, 1 mark for a linked explanation]

4 E.g.
Tennis rackets — newer materials, such as carbon fibre, are lighter, which helps tennis players to move the racket more quickly.
Golf drivers — the shape has been made more aerodynamic, which reduces drag on a swing and helps golfers to generate more power.
[4 marks available — 1 mark for each example, 1 mark for each linked explanation]

5 E.g. it can push them into making decisions based on very fine margins that aren't in the spirit of the game / decisions shown to be wrong by technology can make fans and performers not respect officials.
[2 marks available — 1 mark for each negative effect]

6 (a) E.g. a skinsuit is aerodynamic and allows a cyclist to travel efficiently / a sweat-wicking football shirt remove moisture and keeps a football player dry.
[2 marks available — 1 mark for each example]

(b) E.g. the cost of new technology can be high *[1 mark]*, which means that some performers will not be able to afford it and compete with performers who can *[1 mark]*.

7 E.g.
Effect 1: Reduced excitement for spectators.
Practical example: VAR in football can stop fans from celebrating a goal because it could be overturned.
Effect 2: Spectators may copy poor behaviour.
Practical example: People may see abusive behaviour from spectators on social media and copy it when they watch an event.
[4 marks available — 1 mark for each effect, 1 mark for each linked example]

8 E.g.
Sport: 100 m sprint
Explanation: Running blades allow athletes with limb differences to compete in sprinting events.
[2 marks available — 1 mark for a technology, 1 mark for a linked explanation]

9 E.g.
Technology 1: VAR
How it is used: The video referee in football watches replays and advises the on-field referee of any clear and obvious errors.
Technology 2: DRS
How it is used: The third umpire in cricket reviews decisions using various technologies when the batting team challenges the main umpire's decision.
Technology 3: Hawk-Eye
How it is used: The path of the ball in tennis is tracked, so players can challenge decisions about whether shots are in or out.
[6 marks available — 1 mark for each example, 1 mark for each linked description]

Exam Skills 2

Pages 38–39: Answering 8-Mark Questions

I would give this answer 4 mark(s) out of 8, because it shows good knowledge related to the question, with some development and a sporting example. It doesn't include a justification as to whether PEDs should be used in sport.

Here's an example of an improved answer for the 8-mark question:
Athletes take PEDs for many reasons, despite the fact they can be addictive and lead to some severe health problems, such as strokes.
An athlete may use PEDs to improve an aspect of their fitness, such as strength or speed, which can help them perform better in competitions and win medals or fame. Dwain Chambers, a British 100 m sprinter, took PEDs for this purpose. Young sprinters who looked up to him as a role model could have thought it was OK to take PEDs and copied his behaviour.
Another reason to take PEDs is for faster recovery, which allows an athlete to train more often. Lance Armstrong took PEDs to improve his endurance and recovery, which helped him to win seven Tour de France titles. This gave him an unfair advantage over his competitors. He was eventually caught and stripped of his titles, but it was damaging to the reputation of cycling that he was able to use PEDs for so long.
There are also cases where athletes are pressured into taking PEDs. For example, Shoaib Akhtar, a Pakistani cricketer, said that he was pressured to use PEDs as a teenager to help him bowl faster.
Overall, I feel there is no place for PEDs in sport. An athlete may use them to gain financial rewards and fame, but they can damage their health and reputation. Taking PEDs also goes against the sporting value of fair play.

Mixed Questions

Pages 40-43: Mixed Questions 1

1 (a) E.g.
Barrier 1: Lack of transport
Explanation: She is too young to drive and there may be a lack of public transport to get to her nearest ice rink.
Barrier 2: Lack of awareness of appropriate activity provision
Explanation: She is unfamiliar with the area so may not know where suitable facilities are.
Barrier 3: Lack of appropriate activity provision
Explanation: The ice rink may not offer figure skating sessions at suitable times.
[6 marks available — 1 mark for each barrier to participation, 1 mark for each linked explanation]

(b) Any two from: e.g. provide a minibus or taxi to bring Jas to the ice rink / advertise sessions on social media / offer a range of sessions at a range of times.
   [2 marks available — 1 mark for each action]

2 Sporting initiatives are campaigns which aim to promote sporting activities/values *[1 mark]*. E.g. THIS GIRL CAN is a Sport England initiative that encourages all women and girls to participate in sport *[1 mark]*.

3 (a) Sport: Tennis
   E.g.
   Reason 1: Tennis gets lots of media coverage (e.g. Wimbledon) so many people are aware of it.
   Reason 2: There are a range of tennis role models, so people of different genders and ethnicities will be inspired to take part.
   Reason 3: There are a lot of tennis courts/centres around the UK, so many people have the opportunity to participate.
   [4 marks available — 1 mark for identifying tennis, 1 mark for each reason]

   (b) Any two from: e.g. there are few opportunities for men to participate in netball / netball gets less media coverage than tennis / there are fewer role models for netball than tennis, so fewer people are inspired to play.
   [2 marks available — 1 mark for each reason]

   (c) E.g. I would expect the number of participants to increase *[1 mark]* because emerging sports are ones that are becoming more popular *[1 mark]*.

4 (a) E.g.
   Heart rate monitors — these track a performer's heart rate, so they know if they have been working at the correct intensity or in the correct training zone.
   GPS trackers — these can track average running speed or split times to measure improvements in speed or endurance.
   [4 marks available — 1 mark for each technology, 1 mark for each linked explanation]

   (b) E.g.
   Role 1: To increase the accuracy of officiating.
   Practical example: The TMO in rugby watches video replays to help the on-pitch referee with key decisions.
   Role 2: To increase the safety of performers.
   Practical example: Helmets in BMX protect a performer's head from impact injury.
   [4 marks available — 1 mark for each role of technology, 1 mark for each linked example]
   Enhancing spectatorship is another role you might have identified.

5 (a) E.g. ECB — The Hundred
   [2 marks available — 1 mark for an NGB, 1 mark for a competition/tournament]

   (b) E.g.
   Reason 1: To increase the safety of performers.
   Practical example: The FA banned heading in football training for U12 level and below.
   Reason 2: To make the sport more exciting for spectators.
   Practical example: Table tennis games were made shorter, from 21 points to 11 points.
   [4 marks available — 1 mark for each reason, 1 mark for each linked example]

6 Points you may have written:
   Bidding creates jobs, which can help to boost the country's economy. E.g. many construction workers are needed to build stadiums, hotels and better transport links.
   Bidding can create a legacy of new sporting facilities and infrastructure, which can be used by local people. E.g. venues used for the Sydney Olympic Park are still in use today for sporting and music events.

Bidding brings media attention on the country, which can lead to investment from global companies. E.g. sponsors may spend lots of money on advertising during the Olympic Games, which can help pay towards the event itself.
Bidding is very expensive, which some countries cannot afford, and it is a financial risk for those that can. E.g. England have had two failed bids to host the FIFA World Cup™, costing millions of pounds.
There will be objections to bidding as many people will believe that money could be better invested in other areas of the country or in things like healthcare or education. E.g. other parts of the UK were unhappy that only South East England would benefit from investment at the London 2012 Olympics.
Conclusion: E.g. Bidding for a major sporting event can have more positive than negative effects if the host country can afford to spend the money. It brings employment opportunities and a legacy of improved infrastructure and facilities that would benefit the country, even if the bid fails.
How to grade your answer:

7-8 marks: The answer shows detailed knowledge and understanding. Many developed points are made on the positive and negative effects of bidding for major sporting events, supported with examples. The answer is structured well, uses appropriate terminology, and reaches a justified conclusion.

4-6 marks: The answer shows some good knowledge and understanding. Some developed points are made on the positive and negative effects of bidding for major sporting events, supported with examples. The answer has some structure and uses some appropriate terminology.

1-3 marks: The answer shows only limited knowledge and understanding. Only a few points are made on the positive and negative effects of bidding for major sporting events, with limited or no examples.

0 marks: There is no relevant information.

Pages 44-47: Mixed Questions 2

1 (a) National Governing Bodies are independent organisations that manage a specific sport in a country. *[1 mark]*

   (b) Any two from: e.g. Lawn Tennis Association (LTA) / The Football Association (FA) / England and Wales Cricket Board (ECB) / Rugby Football Union (RFU) / Boccia UK.
   [2 marks available — 1 mark for each NGB]

   (c) Any three from: lobby other organisations for funding / increase participation in their sport / develop coaching qualifications / develop officiating qualifications / ensure safety of all their members / provide support and guidance to their members / organise tournaments and competitions / maintain and enforce the rules of their sport / develop policies and initiatives.
   [3 marks available — 1 mark for each role]

2 (a) E.g. Shin pads protect the legs from impact injuries — a mountain biker wears them to prevent fractures in case they fall off / mouth guards help to absorb the impact when a performer is struck in the face — a hockey player wears one to protect the teeth when struck by a player or hockey stick.
   [4 marks available — 1 mark for each type of equipment, 1 mark for each linked explanation]

   (b) E.g. performers may use cryotherapy/cold chambers. The extremely low temperature restricts blood flow and helps to reduce the swelling around an injury.
   [2 marks available — 1 mark for a technology, 1 mark for a linked description]

Answers

3 (a) Sporting etiquette is the unwritten rules of a sport.
Any two from: it provides a good example to others /
it keeps other performers safe / it promotes sporting
values / it maintains the traditions of the sport.
*[3 marks available — 1 mark for the
description, 1 mark for each reason]*

(b) Any two from: e.g. a football player kicking the ball out
of play when another player is injured / a batter in cricket
admitting the ball touched their bat / a badminton player
acknowledging that their shot went out of the court / players
shaking hands at the start and end of a tennis match.
[2 marks available — 1 mark for each example]

4 (a) Olympic Games: one-off event *[1 mark]*
British Grand Prix: regular and recurring event *[1 mark]*

(b) E.g. Netball World Cup.
It is a one-off event as it happens every four years,
with the host country changing each time.
*[2 marks available — 1 mark for a major sporting event,
1 mark for explaining the type of event]*

5 (a) E.g. an emerging sport is a sport with a low, but rapidly
increasing, number of participants. *[1 mark]*

(b) Any two from: e.g. lacrosse, korfball, kabaddi,
pickleball, padel, ultimate frisbee.
[2 marks available — 1 mark for each sport]

(c) Any two from: e.g. the number of footgolf courses available
/ the number of places to watch footgolf live / the amount
of media coverage of footgolf / sporting successes of
footgolf performers from the UK / the number of footgolf
role models / rainy weather can interrupt footgolf events.
[2 marks available — 1 mark for each factor]

6 (a) E.g. elite performers must provide their location
[1 mark] and give an hour time slot every day
where they available for drug testing *[1 mark]*.

(b) Any two from: e.g. run educational schemes to teach athletes
about the negative effects of PEDs / give sanctions to
discourage the use of PEDs / test athletes before competitions
/ hold an annual Play True Day to promote clean sport.
[2 marks available — 1 mark for each method]

7 Points you may have written:
There are a range of ways that people can access sports
coverage, e.g. TV, radio, newspapers and social media.

Fans can watch many sporting events live or on
catch-up, e.g. Premier League games are shown on
TV subscription channels, such as Sky Sports.

The amount of media coverage varies for different sports,
e.g. Formula One events receive a lot of media coverage,
but skiing events receive very little in the UK.

Media coverage of emerging sports makes people more aware
of them, e.g. skateboarding was featured as an Olympic
sport for the first time at the Tokyo 2020 Olympics.

Media coverage inspires people to participate in sport themselves,
e.g. when Wimbledon is on TV, many people take up tennis.

High level successes attract lots of media attention, increasing
participation or numbers of spectators, e.g. the success of the
England football team in the 2022 UEFA Women's EURO
inspired many women and girls to participate in football.

Media coverage can promote role models who inspire people to
participate, e.g. Emma Raducanu won the US Open, aged 18.
She has inspired many young girls to take up tennis.

<u>Conclusion</u>: E.g. Media coverage has an important role in
increasing the popularity of a sport. The media provides many
options for fans to watch and engage with sport, and also promotes
sporting successes and role models, which increase participation.

How to grade your answer:

7-8 marks: The answer shows detailed knowledge and
understanding. Many developed points are
made on media coverage and how it affects the
popularity of sport, supported with examples.
The answer is structured well, uses appropriate
terminology, and reaches a justified conclusion.

4-6 marks: The answer shows some good knowledge
and understanding. Some developed points
are made on media coverage and how it
affects the popularity of sport, supported with
examples. The answer has some structure
and uses some appropriate terminology.

1-3 marks: The answer shows only limited knowledge and
understanding. Only a few points are made on
media coverage and how it affects the popularity
of sport, with limited or no examples.

0 marks: There is no relevant information.

Pages 48-51: Mixed Questions 3

1 (a) The creed *[1 mark]*
The symbol *[1 mark]*

(b) E.g.
Value: Respect *[1 mark]*
Explanation: Performers should respect other people,
their body and the rules of the sport. *[1 mark]*
Practical example: Simone Biles showed respect to herself
when she pulled out of some gymnastics events at the Tokyo
2020 Olympics to protect her mental health. *[1 mark]*
*You could have written about the value 'excellence' instead,
but not the value 'friendship'. That is an Olympic value,
but the question said you couldn't choose it.*

2 (a) Any two from: e.g. the event is likely to cost more
than it makes / the money spent on hosting the event
should be spent on other needs such as healthcare /
taxes may need to rise to cover the costs of the event.
[2 marks available — 1 mark for each objection]

(b) Any two from: e.g. increased tourism brings
money to the host city / the reputation of the host
city increases, attracting financial investment /
short-term jobs in the host city increases.
[2 marks available — 1 mark for each benefit]

3 (a) E.g.
Barrier 1: Family commitments
Explanation: Donna would need to take care of
her son, so would struggle to participate.
Barrier 2: Lack of transport
Explanation: She doesn't own a car, so would have to rely on
public transport as it is too far to walk to the leisure centre.
*[4 marks available — 1 mark for each barrier,
1 mark for each linked explanation]*
*She is unemployed but the sessions are free, so a lack of
money/disposable income isn't an acceptable answer.*

(b) E.g. the leisure centre could provide a crèche facility to take
care of Donna's child while she participated. *[1 mark]*

(c) Any two from: e.g. use promotional strategies, such
as targeted advertising / promote role models to
inspire people to participate / provide more media
coverage to increase awareness of the sport.
[2 marks available — 1 mark for each way]

4 (a) E.g. officiating technology can slow matches down and
annoy spectators / large screens in the stadium show replays
meaning that spectators do not miss any of the action.
[2 marks available — 1 mark for each way]

Answers

(b) E.g.
Way 1: Social media apps
Advantage: Fans can interact with other fans and express opinions during an event.
Way 2: Websites
Advantage: Fans can get score updates on their smartphones while they are out doing other things.
[4 marks available — 1 mark for each way, 1 mark for each linked advantage]

5 (a) World Anti-Doping Agency (WADA) *[1 mark]*

   (b) Any two from: e.g. issuing sanctions, such as bans or fines, to performers found to have taken PEDs / using education strategies to encourage clean sport / drug testing (WADA's Whereabouts Rule) so elite performers know they could easily be caught.
   [2 marks available — 1 mark for each approach]

6 Points you may have written:

NGBs use promotional schemes to increase the number of participants in their sport. E.g. Basketball England has a SLAM JAM programme to provide fun basketball experiences to primary school pupils in order to encourage them to participate.

NGBs develop policies that focus on equal opportunities and inclusion. This increases participation from certain groups, e.g. ethnic minorities.

NGBs have levelled coaching and officiating qualifications, e.g. England Handball has Level 1 and 2 awards for both coaching and officiating. This increases the number of training sessions or tournaments that can run and the opportunities for participation.

NGBs use initiatives to encourage participation. E.g. one aim of the FA's 'Survive. Revive. Thrive.' initiative is to increase the number of women participating in football.

Funding raised through lobbying can be put towards initiatives to encourage participation. Funding is also used to pay elite performers who ultimately increase participation if they act as inspirational role models.

Other functions of an NGB include maintaining or adapting the rules of a sport, organising tournaments, providing support to members and ensuring the safety of its members, e.g. through safeguarding policies.

Conclusion: E.g. I think the statement is true. A sport would not exist without participants, so promoting participation is vital. Even the functions of an NGB that are not directly aimed at increasing participation often help to do so indirectly. For example, increasing safety could encourage more parents to let their children take part in the sport.

How to grade your answer:

7-8 marks: The answer shows detailed knowledge and understanding. Many developed points are made on the functions of NGBs, supported with examples. The answer is structured well, uses appropriate terminology, and reaches a justified conclusion.

4-6 marks: The answer shows some good knowledge and understanding. Some developed points are made on the functions of NGBs, supported with examples. The answer has some structure and uses some appropriate terminology.

1-3 marks: The answer shows only limited knowledge and understanding. Only a few points are made on the functions of NGBs, with limited or no examples.

0 marks: There is no relevant information.

Pages 52-55: Mixed Questions 4

1 (a) Any two from: e.g. teenager / carer / people with family commitments.
   [2 marks available — 1 mark for each user group]

   (b) Any two from: e.g. he has family commitments / he has a lack of time / he may have a lack of transport / he may have a lack of disposable income.
   [3 marks available — 1 mark for each barrier]

   (c) E.g. Billy could get a family member to look after his dad in the evenings, which would give him time to take part in sport with his friends.
   Local sports facilities could introduce subsidised sessions to help Billy afford the sessions.
   Billy's college could offer sessions at lunch times, which means he could take part in sport at times when he doesn't need to care for his dad.
   [3 marks available — 1 mark for each solution]

2 Any two from: e.g.
Clothing/footwear — examples include aerodynamic swimsuits, spiked shoes, thermals.
Training analysis equipment — examples include smartwatches, heart rate monitors, GPS vests.
Assistive technology — examples include prosthetics, sports wheelchairs, balls for goalball.
[4 marks available — 1 mark for each type, 1 mark for each linked example]

3 Any two from: e.g.
A regular event is hosted in a different city each year — examples include The OPEN® Championship and UEFA Champions League Final.
A regular and recurring event is hosted in the same city each year — examples include Wimbledon and the Formula 1 British Grand Prix.
A one-off event happens less often than annually. A city won't host again for a long period of time — examples include the Olympic Games and the Commonwealth Games.
[4 marks available — 1 mark for each description, 1 mark for each named example]

4 (a) Inspiration: e.g. Paralympic athletes are role models for many spectators, who may be encouraged to participate themselves.
   Determination: e.g. Paralympic athletes have to overcome many barriers to compete at the highest level.
   Equality: e.g. Paralympic athletes showcase and celebrate people's differences and promote inclusion in sport.
   [3 marks available — 1 mark for each description]

   (b) Excellence, respect, friendship.
   [3 marks available — 1 mark for each value]

5 (a) E.g.
Technology 1: Hawk-Eye
Practical example: Hawk-Eye is used to show the path of the ball in tennis when a player challenges the umpire's decision.
Technology 2: VAR
Practical example: VAR in football is an off-field referee who watches slow-motion replays to advise the on-field referee of any 'clear and obvious' errors.
[4 marks available — 1 mark for each technology, 1 mark for each linked description]

   (b) Any one from: e.g. games are stopped to allow reviews to take place / players and spectators may not respect officials if their decisions are proven to be wrong by technology / officials can be influenced by technology and not rely on their own decisions. *[1 mark]*

Answers

6   (a) E.g. the LTA (NGB for tennis) could:
develop training of elite performers by setting up a national
centre of excellence for tennis / develop training of
officials by providing levelled courses / develop the skills
of coaches at all levels by providing levelled courses.
[2 marks available — 1 mark for a way,
1 mark for a linked example]

     (b) Any three from: e.g. hold fundraising events / contact
brands for sponsorship deals / collect membership
fees / sell merchandise / apply for National Lottery
grants / apply for Sport England grants.
[3 marks available — 1 mark for each way]

7   Points you may have written:

Athletes use PEDs to increase their fitness and improve
performance. E.g. Marion Jones admitted to using PEDs to
improve her sprinting performance. Her decision to use PEDs may
have been influenced by other performers using PEDs at the time.

Athletes use PEDs to win competitions and gain money,
through financial awards and sponsorship deals. E.g.
Lance Armstrong used PEDs to win many Tour de France
titles, gaining lucrative sponsorship deals with NIKE.

PEDs can damage the reputation of many performers.
E.g. 100 m sprinter Justin Gatlin would have lost respect
from many fans after testing positive for PED use.

PEDs can damage the reputation of sport and fans may start
to question the results of sporting events. E.g. Russia were
accused of a doping program and stripped of Olympic medals,
which could lead to a decrease in spectators at the Olympics.

PEDs pose many health risks to athletes and can be addictive.
E.g. there are physical health risks such as strokes/high blood
pressure, and mental health risks such as depression.

<u>Conclusion</u>: E.g. Some athletes may argue PEDs only
offer a minimal advantage to performance, just like using
technology. However, many athletes believe PEDs undermine
the spirit of sport and it goes against the sporting value of
fair play. There are health risks and sanctions associated
with PEDs, so athletes should avoid taking them.

How to grade your answer:

7-8 marks: The answer shows detailed knowledge and
understanding. Many developed points are
made on the positive and negative effects of
PEDs, supported with examples. The answer is
structured well, uses appropriate terminology,
and reaches a justified conclusion.

4-6 marks: The answer shows some good knowledge and
understanding. Some developed points are made
on the positive and negative effects of PEDs,
supported with examples. The answer has some
structure and uses some appropriate terminology.

1-3 marks: The answer shows only limited knowledge
and understanding. Only a few points are
made on the positive and negative effects
of PEDs, with limited or no examples.

0 marks: There is no relevant information.

Pages 56-59: Mixed Questions 5

1   (a) Any three from: e.g. she may have a lack of disposable
income / she may lack positive sporting role models / she may
have a lack of transport / there may be a lack of appropriate
provision if sessions are only on when she is studying.
[3 marks available — 1 mark for each barrier]

     (b) Any two from: e.g.
Lack of disposable income — appropriate pricing,
including concessions for students, would make
sessions more affordable for Roberta.

Lack of positive sporting role models — targeted promotions
using teenagers/students as role models would give Roberta
someone to look up to and give her confidence to take part.

Lack of time — having sessions at a range of times
would allow Roberta to participate in squash around
the hours she is studying or looking for a job.
[4 marks available — 1 mark for each solution,
1 mark for each linked explanation]

2   (a) Following unwritten rules/conventions when watching sport.
[1 mark]

     (b) Any three from: e.g. cheering on a team or performer
/ applauding fair play / remaining silent when
expected / respecting other national anthems.
[3 marks available — 1 mark for each example]

3   (a) Local, regional, national.
[3 marks available — 1 mark for each]

     (b) E.g.
Sporting initiative: Chance to Shine
Aim: This initiative works with organisations to give
children the opportunity to play cricket in school.
[2 marks available — 1 mark for a sporting initiative,
1 mark for the aim]
You don't need to know every sporting initiative out there,
but make sure you know the key facts about at least
one from each level (local, regional and national).

4   (a) Any three from: e.g. improved infrastructure /
increase in short-term employment / increased
tourism / increased global reputation.
[3 marks available — 1 mark for each benefit]

     (b) Any two from: e.g. potential for increased crime and
terrorism / increased traffic congestion / increased amount of
litter / negative media coverage on failures of the event.
[2 marks available — 1 mark for each problem]

5   (a) Any two from: e.g. to recover faster from injury / to
reduce pain / to improve performance / to improve
an aspect of their fitness / because of pressure to
succeed / to gain financial rewards or fame.
[2 marks available — 1 mark for each reason]

     (b) Any three from: e.g. they damage health / it is unfair
on other athletes who follow the rules / it goes against
sporting values / people who see them as a role model
may copy their behaviour / they may get banned
from competing / they may damage their reputation
/ they may damage the reputation of the sport.
[3 marks available — 1 mark for each reason]

6   E.g.
Factor 1: The provision of facilities.
Explanation: The UK has many football pitches,
so there are many opportunities to participate.
Factor 2: The high level success of teams and individuals.
Explanation: The success of the England women's
team has inspired many girls to participate.
[4 marks available — 1 mark for each factor,
1 mark for each linked explanation]

7   Points you may have written:

Technology can keep elite performers safe and reduce
their chances of injury, e.g. smart mouthguards are being
introduced for rugby players to detect head injuries.

Technology is used to analyse elite performers during training
to help coaches work out the areas of fitness or skills that a
performer needs to improve, e.g. heart rate monitors show
the intensity a hockey player is working at during training.

Technology can speed up recovery from injuries, so
elite performers can return to competitions quickly, e.g.

Answers

long-distance runners may use hyperbaric chambers to reduce the swelling from a sprained foot.

New materials for clothing can enhance performance, so elite performers may achieve new records in their sport, e.g. skinsuits for track cycling reduce air resistance and give marginal gains.

Technology can be very expensive which gives wealthy performers/clubs an advantage over less wealthy performers/clubs. E.g. indoor golf simulators can cost thousands of pounds.

The use of video replays in sports such as rugby can slow the game down, making it less appealing to spectators which could decrease the number of spectators of elite level sport.

Officials could be influenced by technology to change their decisions. For example, a football VAR official may put pressure on the on-field referee to review a decision they made.

Conclusion: E.g. Technology can result in inequality between performers/clubs, but I feel its value in improving performance at the elite level outweighs this. I feel it is important for officials to make correct decisions, even if this slows down the game for spectators. Therefore, I think that technology in sport has an overall positive effect at the elite level.

How to grade your answer:

7-8 marks: The answer shows detailed knowledge and understanding. Many developed points are made on the positive and negative impacts of technology in elite sport, supported with examples. The answer is structured well, uses appropriate terminology, and reaches a justified conclusion.

4-6 marks: The answer shows some good knowledge and understanding. Some developed points are made on the positive and negative impacts of technology in elite sport, supported with examples. The answer has some structure and uses some appropriate terminology.

1-3 marks: The answer shows only limited knowledge and understanding. Only a few points are made on the positive and negative impacts of technology in elite sport, with limited or no examples.

0 marks: There is no relevant information.

Pages 60-63: Mixed Questions 6

1 (a) Any one from: e.g.
Family commitments — Ronnie cannot participate in sessions outside school hours as he needs to look after his children.
Lack of appropriate activity provision — the sessions offered during school hours are high-intensity, so they are not suitable for someone with low fitness.
[2 marks available — 1 mark for a barrier, 1 mark for a linked explanation]

 (b) Any two from: e.g. provide a crèche so that he could participate out of school hours / provide family sessions so he could participate with his children / provide low-intensity sessions during school hours.
[2 marks available — 1 mark for each solution]

 (c) Any one from: e.g. providing a crèche would mean more staffing costs / other classes might be cancelled so that a suitable class for Ronnie can run which could affect the profits of the centre. *[1 mark]*

2 (a) Any two from: e.g. training coaches to teach participants safe techniques / adapting rules to reduce the chances of injuries / using sanctions to deter people from breaking safety rules / providing advice on equipment to be used by different ages / creating safeguarding policies to protect vulnerable participants.
[2 marks available — 1 mark for each way]

 (b) Any three from: e.g. promoting clubs and teams / creating safeguarding policies / providing funding for facilities / advising members on insurance / giving technical guidance to clubs.
[3 marks available — 1 mark for each way]

3 (a) Sportsmanship is being honest and sticking to the rules / playing within the letter and spirit of the sport.
E.g. congratulating an opponent's shot in golf / kicking the ball out of play when a football player is injured / shaking hands with an opponent in tennis / showing respect to an umpire in hockey.
[3 marks available — 1 mark for explaining the term, 1 mark for each linked example]

 (b) Gamesmanship is bending the rules to gain an advantage.
E.g. a footballer delaying the taking of a corner to waste time / exaggerating an injury to increase the chance of a foul being given in netball / sledging in cricket to intimidate opponents.
[3 marks available — 1 mark for explaining the term, 1 mark for each linked example]

4 (a) An international sporting event has participants and spectators from two or more countries. E.g. the Olympic Games has participants and spectators from all over the world.
[2 marks available — 1 mark for a description, 1 mark for a linked example]

 (b) Regular, regular and recurring, one-off.
[3 marks available — 1 mark for each type]

5 (a) E.g. spectators are more engaged in the game / spectators have a greater understanding of why the referee has made a decision, so they trust officials more.
[2 marks available — 1 mark for each positive impact]

 (b) E.g.
Way 1: Instant in-depth analysis increases interest.
Example: Possession data in football is instantly available.
Way 2: There is a large amount of coverage of all sports on the internet.
Example: A fan of a less popular sport in the UK, such as sumo wrestling, can watch it live.
[4 marks available — 1 mark for each way, 1 mark for each linked example]

6 Points you may have written:

A major sporting event can make a profit, e.g. the Los Angeles 1984 Olympics was profitable. This profit can be reinvested back into the country, e.g. to improve transport systems.

However, in many cases, sporting events make a financial loss, e.g. the Athens 2004 Olympics made a loss which negatively impacted the Greek economy.

A major sporting event can leave a positive sporting legacy. Facilities built for the event can be used by locals and increase participation in sport, e.g. the Copper Box Arena was built for the London 2012 Olympics and is now used by the community.

However, some facilities built for an event are found to be too expensive to run and are left unused. E.g. the aquatics centre built for the Rio 2016 Olympics was abandoned after just nine months.

Increased media attention from hosting a major sporting event can increase tourism in the city or country, bringing in money and boosting the economy. It can also increase the host's reputation, attracting investment from global companies.

However, some events attract negative media coverage, which damages the host's global reputation. E.g. there were stories on social media about unsafe weather and poor living conditions at the Beijing 2022 Winter Olympics.

Answers

<u>Conclusion</u>: E.g. Hosting a major sporting event is very risky. Most countries spend more than they earn from hosting an event and have debts to repay, which outweighs the positive impacts. *You could have drawn the opposite conclusion, as long as you supported your answer.*

How to grade your answer:

7-8 marks: The answer shows detailed knowledge and understanding. Many developed points are made on the post-event positive and negative impacts of hosting a major sporting event, supported with examples. The answer is structured well, uses appropriate terminology, and reaches a justified conclusion.

4-6 marks: The answer shows some good knowledge and understanding. Some developed points are made on the post-event positive and negative impacts of hosting a major sporting event, supported with examples. The answer has some structure and uses some appropriate terminology.

1-3 marks: The answer shows only limited knowledge and understanding. Only a few points are made on the post-event positive and negative impacts of hosting a major sporting event, with limited or no examples.

0 marks: There is no relevant information.

Pages 64-67: Mixed Questions 7

1 (a) E.g.
Basketball: Lack of transport — 15 miles is too far to walk, so John would rely on his family to take him.
Rugby union: Lack of disposable income — each session costs £8, which may be more than John's family can afford.
Handball: Lack of appropriate activity provision — John is likely to be at school at 2 pm on a Tuesday.
Lacrosse: Lack of disposable income — John's family may not be able to afford to buy him a lacrosse stick.
[4 marks available — 1 mark for each barrier]

   (b) Any three from: e.g. organise transport to take him to the basketball club / have concession pricing for children attending rugby union / put on a wider range of session times for handball / have free equipment hire for lacrosse.
[3 marks available — 1 mark for each solution]

2 E.g. performers may make mistakes — shouting at a snooker player as they take a shot could distract them and cause them to miss / it could result in an unfair game — abusive chants by spectators at a football match can distract players, giving the opposing team an advantage.
[4 marks available — 1 mark for each consequence, 1 mark for each linked example]

3 Any one from: e.g. there are more people spending money in the city, which is good for businesses / there are more temporary jobs created, e.g. in hotels / transport infrastructure is improved to cope with the extra people.
Any one from: e.g. there will be more litter / increased risk of crime or terrorism / increased congestion on roads.
[2 marks available — 1 mark for each aspect]

4 Any two from: e.g. provide pool hoists for people with physical impairments / provide ramps for wheelchair users / provide hearing loops for people with hearing impairments / provide Braille signage for partially-sighted users.
[2 marks available — 1 mark for each action]

5 (a) E.g.
NGB: Great Britain Wheelchair Rugby *[1 mark]*
Sport: Wheelchair rugby *[1 mark]*

   (b) E.g. Great Britain Wheelchair Rugby could: advertise in the media to increase awareness of their sport / develop schemes and initiatives to encourage people with physical impairments to participate.
[2 marks available — 1 mark for each way]

   (c) NGBs can offer levelled training course for coaches *[1 mark]*. E.g. England Handball offers a Level 1 and Level 2 award in coaching *[1 mark]*.

6 (a) E.g.
Positive impact: it can increase the accuracy of the decisions made by officials.
Negative impact: it can be expensive, so there is unequal access between wealthy and poorer clubs/performers.
[2 marks available — 1 mark for each impact]

   (b) E.g. cryotherapy — cold temperatures help to reduce swelling from a muscle sprain.
[2 marks available — 1 mark for a technology, 1 mark for a linked description]

7 Points you may have written:
Lack of sessions at suitable times affects both groups. Both teenagers and adults cannot participate in sport when they are in school or at work. Teenagers also have homework which takes up time after school but some adults work shifts which affects their ability to participate at a regular time.

Many sports sessions are either for children or adults, so teenagers might not feel comfortable in either. However, there are PE sessions and clubs linked to schools, which would give teenagers the opportunity to participate.

Most adults have some disposable income to participate in sport, but teenagers tend to have less and rely on their family, so a lack of disposable income affects teenagers more than adults.

Most teenagers don't drive, but many adults do. Therefore, a lack of transport is generally a bigger barrier for teenagers than adults.

Many adults are parents, so generally have more family commitments than teenagers. Parents may require childcare to participate in sport, which can be expensive.

<u>Conclusion</u>: E.g. I think adults have more barriers to participation than teenagers as they generally have more responsibilities, such as work and family. Also, teenagers have the opportunity to participate through school, which adults don't have, so they have to search for suitable sessions themselves.
You could have drawn the opposite conclusion, as long as you supported your answer.

How to grade your answer:

7-8 marks: The answer shows detailed knowledge and understanding. Many developed points are made on the barriers to participation faced by teenagers and adults, supported with examples. The answer is structured well, uses appropriate terminology, and reaches a justified conclusion.

4-6 marks: The answer shows some good knowledge and understanding. Some developed points are made on the barriers to participation faced by teenagers and adults, supported with examples. The answer has some structure and uses some appropriate terminology.

1-3 marks: The answer shows only limited knowledge and understanding. Only a few points are made on the barriers to participation faced by teenagers and adults, with limited or no examples.

0 marks: There is no relevant information.